Productivity
and
Higher Education

Productivity
and
Higher Education

Improving the Effectiveness
of Faculty, Facilities,
and Financial Resources

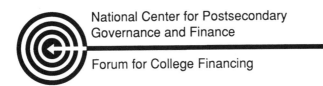

National Center for Postsecondary
Governance and Finance

Forum for College Financing

Richard E. Anderson and Joel W. Meyerson
Editors

Peterson's Guides
Princeton, New Jersey

Library of Congress Cataloging-in-Publication Data

Productivity and higher education : improving the effectiveness of faculty, facilities, and financial resources / Richard E. Anderson and Joel W. Meyerson, editors.
    p. cm.
Includes bibliographical references.
ISBN 1-56079-090-3
1. Universities and colleges—United States—Business management.
2. Universities and colleges—United States—Administration.
3. College facilities—United States. I. Anderson, Richard E., 1943– .
II. Meyerson, Joel W., 1951– .
LB2341.95.U6P76   1991
378.73—dc20   91-22290

Composition and design by Peterson's Guides

Printed in the United States of America

10   9   8   7   6   5   4   3   2   1

Contents

Contributors —————————————

Editors

Richard E. Anderson has been vice chancellor for finance at Washington University since 1990. Prior to this appointment, he was the chairman of and a professor in the department of higher and adult education at Columbia University Teachers College. He has written and coedited a number of books and monographs on the subject of financial planning and higher education. *Productivity and Higher Education* is his fourth collaboration with Joel W. Meyerson.

Joel W. Meyerson is partner and director of the higher education and non-profit practices of Coopers & Lybrand. He codirected the Forum for College Financing with Richard E. Anderson and has served on many advisory panels concerned with finance and higher education. Meyerson is the author and coauthor of a number of books on economics and higher education including *Strategic Analysis: Using Comparative Data to Understand Your Institution* and *Higher Education in a Changing Economy.*

Essayists

Robert Birnbaum is professor of higher education at the University of Maryland College Park. He has previously served as vice chancellor of the City University of New York, vice chancellor of the New Jersey Department of Higher Education, and chancellor of the University of Wisconsin–Oshkosh. Birnbaum's research findings appear regularly in higher education journals, and he is the recipient of the annual Research Achievement Award of the Association for the Study of Higher Education. His latest book, *Renewing Institutional Leadership,* will be published in 1992.

John T. Hackett's career spans both industry and academia. He is currently managing general partner at Indianapolis-based CID Venture Partners, L.P. Before accepting this position in July 1991, he served for three years as vice president of finance and administration at Indiana University Bloomington. His teaching experience includes faculty positions at I.U., Ohio State University, Case Western Reserve University, and Kent State University. In industry, he has been an economist and a chief financial officer. As a speaker and writer, Hackett has addressed professional and academic groups and contributed to various journals on the subject of financial management.

George R. Houston Jr. is senior vice president and treasurer of Georgetown University, where he is also assistant professor of accounting—a position he has held since 1966. At Georgetown, Houston, who is a CPA, developed a number of business courses, including a fifteen-month graduate program leading to a Master of Science in accounting. His career at the university includes the posts of acting vice president for business and finance and vice president for financial affairs. Active in many higher education administration–oriented organizations, he has delivered papers on such diverse topics as financial officers' perspectives of higher education, governance of private universities, and investment polices for nonprofit organizations.

Harvey H. Kaiser is a senior vice president at Syracuse University with primary responsibility for facilities administration. He is also an associate professor of urban planning in the Maxwell School of Citizenship and Public Affairs. Kaiser, who is a registered architect, holds a master's degree in urban planning and a Ph.D in social sciences. He has written and lectured extensively on the subject of higher education facilities management and historic architectural preservation and has been a facilities-management consultant to higher education associations, statewide public systems, and individual campuses in the United States, Canada, and Israel.

Edward L. MacCordy is associate vice chancellor for research at Washington University, a post he has held since 1976. Active in professional associations, MacCordy has been the president of the National Council of University Research Administrators and the Association of University Technology Managers. He has been a member of the National Institutes of Health's Biomedical Research Support Review Subcommittee, the Department of Commerce's Advisory Committee on Patent Law Reform, the Council of Governmental Relations, and the Licensing Executives Society. He received a Bachelor of Science in civil engineering from Tufts University and a master's degree in management and industrial engineering from Rensselaer Polytechnic Institute.

William F. Massy is the director of the Stanford Institute for Higher Education Research and heads the higher education program in administration and policy analysis at the Stanford School of Education. He is also professor of education and business administration at the university. He was the university's chief financial officer from 1990 to 1991, vice president for finance from 1989 to 1990, vice president for business and finance from 1977 to 1989, vice provost for research from 1971 to 1977, and associate dean of the Stanford Graduate School of Business in 1971. He is author and coauthor of several books, including *Planning Models for Colleges and Universities* and *Stochastic Models of Buying Behavior,* and numerous journal articles.

John H. Pencavel is professor of economics at Stanford University, a position he has held since 1969, and, since 1986, he has also been the editor of the American Economic Association's *Journal of Economic Literature.* He received undergraduate and master's degrees from the University of London and earned a Ph.D from Princeton University. Pencavel's works include the recently published book *Labor Markets Under Trade Unionism: Employment, Wages, and Hours* as well as numerous journal articles, book reviews, and commentaries.

Sean C. Rush is a partner in Coopers & Lybrand's national higher education consulting practice. He has more than sixteen years of administrative, consulting, and policy-level experience with colleges and universities, state government, health-care institutions, and service-sector companies. He has been involved in financial planning, operations management and improvement, organizational analysis, management auditing strategies, mergers, and business planning. His clients have included Harvard University, Pennsylvania State University, Boston University, the Texas Select Committee on Higher Education, and the Arizona Board of Regents.

Stephen Joel Trachtenberg has been the president of George Washington University since 1988. Prior to accepting this position, he was, for eleven years, the president of the University of Hartford and professor of law and public administration. Before assuming the presidency of Hartford, Trachtenberg served for eight years at Boston University as dean and vice president. Earlier, during the Lyndon B. Johnson administration, he had been a special assistant to the U.S. Education Commissioner in the Department of Health, Education, and Welfare. In that period he also served as secretary for a White House task force on education. An outspoken advocate of higher eduction, Trachtenberg has written extensively on the subject and has testified before the U.S. Congress.

Introduction

Productivity or Quality?

Sean C. Rush

Partner, Higher Education Consulting Services
Coopers & Lybrand

During the past several years, the word productivity has crept into the lexicon of higher education with all the subtlety of a Kansas tornado. Previously an anathema at most institutions, the term is now bandied about with considerable urgency as institution after institution grapples with shrinking resources and growing budget shortfalls. Downsizing, retrenchment, and doing more with less have become themes, if not necessities, for most institutions. However, despite the frequent use of the word productivity on many campuses, its actual meaning, acceptance, and application within higher education is less than clear.

The notion of productivity brings substantial baggage with it. All but the most steely hearts shudder at the thought of a productivity initiative in their workplace. For many, the word itself conjures up images of Taloresque time-and-motion studies, sweat-inducing taskmasters, or Charlie Chaplin forever caught in the gears of a gargantuan machine in the 1936 movie *Modern Times*. For most people, productivity, like reading Tolstoy's *War and Peace*, is something more often talked about than actually done.

Within higher education, the practical implementation of the concept is especially nettlesome. As Robert Birnbaum points out in Chapter 2, "The perceived lack of productivity in higher education may lie less with our institutions and more with our measurements: money may not be the best measure of the value of services." How does one value the intellectual ex-

The author would like to thank Jennifer Dowling, Johna McFarland, Loren Loomis Hubbell, and Daphne Kempner, all of Coopers & Lybrand, for their contributions to this chapter.

change between a student and teacher? A basic discovery in a campus laboratory? An institutional public-service initiative? Because the primary purpose of colleges and universities is the creation and transfer of knowledge and *not* the maximization of shareholder wealth, many monetary measures of performance fall short.

PRODUCTIVITY HAS NOT BEEN A CONCERN

Part of the problem of productivity in higher education may be that colleges and universities have not had to cope with the issue. For the past forty years, higher education has been an extraordinary growth industry. Since 1950

- total enrollment in American colleges and universities has grown more than 400 percent, from 2.7 million to the current 13 million;
- the total number of institutions has grown by more than 80 percent, from 1,800 to 3,300; and
- college and university facility space has increased by more than 500 percent, growing from 500 million to some 3 *billion* square feet of space.

Between 1955 and 1974, a new institution was opened at the rate of one every two weeks. More college and university space was constructed during this period than in the preceding 200 years. These statistics are not the telltale signs of an ailing industry. The main problem during this period was coping with incredible growth, not retrenchment.

During that four-decade stretch, a substantial number of institutions became large, highly complex, businesses. Although many within the industry rail at the thought, higher education is a big business with some institutional budgets well in excess of $1 billion—easily cracking *Fortune* magazine's 500 companies in terms of financial size. The first inkling of the business aspect of higher education may well have surfaced in the turn-of-the-century observations of Arthur Twining Hadley, president of Yale between 1899 and 1921. He commented that when he visited Noah Porter (Yale president, 1881–86), he would find him reading *Kant* in his *study,* but when he visited Porter's successor, Timothy Dwight, he found that president examining *balance sheets* in his *office.* Since then, the business of higher education has grown into a sizable industry. In aggregate, American higher education

- spends approximately $120 billion in operating expenses (excluding capital),

- has a physical-plant replacement value of some $300 billion,
- manages more than $75 billion in endowment funds, and
- employs millions of faculty members and staff.

Today's research university is a far cry from its ancestors, the small medieval colleges of masters, teachers, and students. It offers a dazzling array of classrooms, laboratories, housing, museums, galleries, gymnasia, technology, and support services. In short, many universities have become self-contained small cities as more and more functions become integrated into the enterprise. As John Hackett points out in Chapter 6, this vertical integration adds both complexity and cost to institutional budgets but has also become the norm.

Hence, as colleges and universities move through the 1990s, they've come from a period of unprecedented growth in size, complexity, and sophistication. The challenges of the prior forty years were less about costs and productivity and more about keeping pace with the surging demand for higher education.

A New Environment

Despite the seeming prosperity of the late 1970s and early 1980s, higher education was also filled with a number of would-be Cassandras. Various doom-and-gloom scenarios were prophesied based on changing demographics and uncertain national economic performance. Yet, despite the dour forecasts, the 1980s proved to be a relatively prosperous time for higher education. Resourceful management tapped new student markets to increase the nontraditional-age student pool, robust economic performance bolstered endowments and spurred charitable giving, and low inflation kept at least some operating costs in line.

This period of prosperity, however, masked a number of fundamental problems. Expenses increased, enabled by revenue growth that has since proved unsustainable. New education program initiatives and burgeoning academic support were built while the ever-increasing cost of maintenance of educational facilities was deferred. The delicate balance between trends in institutional resources and needs and between long- and short-term interests was tipped into financial disequilibrium at many institutions by the late 1980s. The Cassandras had finally hit pay dirt!

Administrators must now address budget gaps caused by constricted institutional resource growth and burgeoning needs. National and regional economic recessions make traditional external funding sources uncertain.

Finally, changing student demographics present new concerns during a time of growing public concern and focus on the price and value of higher education.

Finite Resources

Several factors contribute to the rising concern over resources and revenues in higher education, including tuition, federal and state aid, state tax revenues, federal research grants, and a cooling economy.

Tuition charges at most private institutions grew at yearly rates of 8 to 11 percent in the 1980s, well ahead of the national inflation rate and outpacing increases in median family income. There is both a growing public resistance to the trend of steep tuition increases and a fairly pervasive sense in the education industry that the pace of tuition growth must slow down.

The problem of rapid tuition growth outstripping families' ability to pay has been compounded by declining federally funded student aid. The burden of financial aid has increasingly passed to the institutions, resulting in a 130 percent increase in institutionally funded student aid from 1980 to 1988. This institutionally funded aid directly offsets tuition revenue and causes institutions to retain less of each incremental tuition revenue dollar and further squeezes institutions' resources.

At a macro level, states are at a twelve-year low for year-end financial reserves, making it difficult to withstand an economic downturn. Hence, colleges and universities can expect declining allocations of tax revenues as states struggle to do more with less.

In addition, competition for federal research dollars has grown. Although the government is still the most significant source of research funding, its largesse slowed considerably in the 1980s, especially compared with the quickening pace of other research funding sources. Academic institutions and the private sector are assuming a greater share of the nation's research efforts. The shift away from federal funding hurts colleges in two ways: first, to the extent that institutions move toward self-funding the direct costs of research, their level of expenditure on research will rise; second, research grants from private foundations and companies generally do not fund indirect costs. As institutions and the private sector finance more of the direct and indirect costs of research, fewer discretionary revenue sources are left to finance other educational activities.

Lastly, as the economy has slowed down, charitable giving has leveled in real terms. Further, erratic endowment performance has mirrored the economic uncertainty and market volatility that have prevailed since 1987.

These financial-resource issues present real and immediate problems to college and university administrators, who also face problems of expanding needs.

Expanding Needs

In an era when quality was defined under the more-is-better model, colleges and universities grew, expanding programs, scholarships, and student services as they went. Budgeting was at the margin: How much more can we do/offer this year? Now institutions are faced with an altogether different task—budgeting the core programs. The questions are different now: How will we fund the institution we've become? What is central to our mission?

A number of needs have emerged as critical only recently in higher education. An aging work force, government intervention, sophisticated technology, declining enrollment, and long-deferred maintenance present unique demands to administrators.

Generally, personnel costs comprise nearly 70 percent of an institution's operating budget. Over the last eight years, faculty salaries, one of the largest components of compensation expense, have risen faster than inflation. Yet despite high investment in this area in the 1980s, faculty still have not regained the salary purchasing power they had in the 1960s and early 1970s. Furthermore, while salaries have always been a large part of the university budget, its portion could grow dramatically as institutions are forced to offer more money to attract top candidates from the declining number of doctoral students.

Fringe benefits are also increasingly costly to institutions. Health-care costs have escalated and increased the cost of medical benefits. In 1994, retirement benefits will prove to be particularly challenging as mandatory retirement will be eliminated by law. The aging faculty work force not only will increase the duration of the institution's pension-fund contributions but also will preclude younger, less expensive faculty appointments.

Government regulation and taxation also present growing expenses to universities. For example, demonstrating and reporting compliance on such issues as primate care in biomedical research will increase the cost of doing that research. In addition, lawmakers increasingly view higher education as a potential source of new tax revenue. Changes to the unrelated-business income tax (UBIT) will tax more directly activities—such as bookstores, travel and tour groups, food services, and hotels—run by colleges and universities. Another area under review as a source of new tax revenue is endowment income. Legislation of this type would directly affect the institution's operating expenses.

Cost concerns have also increased in the areas of obtaining and maintaining scientific equipment, computers, and other technology. The growing sophistication of technology in recent years presents unique needs, often requiring special facilities, maintenance, and ongoing technical support. Institutions are called upon to provide the most up-to-date resources and associated support services as possible, as part of a high-quality education. Yet, the prohibitive cost of obtaining and maintaining these state-of-the-art technologies means that most institutions just haven't been able to keep up. Despite major investments in this area, most college and university labs are stacked with equipment that is old and technological-generations out of date.

The declining applicant pool also presents unique requirements. Recruitment costs, including market analysis, marketing consultants, and direct-mail campaigns, are becoming significant cost factors. This is particularly true in minority recruiting. Recruitment for qualified minority students is intense. Furthermore, proportionately, minority students have historically needed more financial aid support. The greatest opportunities for maintaining enrollment levels lie in increasing minority enrollment, yet this presents even more financial challenges to institutions.

The thread of consistency among these issues is the rigorous challenge of maintaining or increasing quality while decreasing cost. Shrinking revenue streams and upward pressures on costs are forcing college and university leaders to think of ways to do more with less. One college financial officer remarked, "How can we look so rich and feel so poor?" For many people, this translates into achieving greater productivity, and therein lies the rub. As Stephen Trachtenberg points out in Chapter 1, academics argue over how to define or measure productivity but feel that the concept of productivity should be left in the corporate sector.

LONG-TERM PROBLEMS, SHORT-TERM SOLUTIONS

Higher education's response to its budgetary shortfalls has been predictable. The most common reactions include

- hiring and spending freezes,

- across-the-board budget cuts (usually by some percentage amount), and
- reductions in force (RIFs) or layoffs.

The difficulty with most of these approaches is that they are often short-term solutions—sometimes damaging to the institution and frequently harmful to institutional morale. The words used to describe these initiatives connote failure. Downsizing and retrenchment are not words of optimism. However, despite the negative aura surrounding these activities, downsizing usually does occur. As William Massy and Robert Zemsky have pointed out in "The Lattice and the Ratchet," published in the June 1990 issue of *Policy Perspectives,* most departments will chip in with budget freezes or reductions to help address the problem at hand. When the problems appear to have passed, budgets quickly return to their original size as pent-up needs are funded and reintroduced into the operating budget. In most instances, institutions do not fundamentally rethink their current position and put in place lasting, long-term corrective solutions. Too often, the issue is viewed as a short-term problem rather than an opportunity to change the culture and overcome inertia.

Any college or university that views the current issues and problems as short term has misread the socioeconomic tea leaves. Most of the problems predicted for the 1980s have come to pass, albeit ten years late. The key concern for higher education is to recognize the permanence of these issues. Short-term solutions to long-term problems will not suffice. The challenge is not how to merely survive with fewer funds in the future but how to thrive with less money.

Begin with Quality, Not Productivity

As institutions of higher education attempt to cope with the many cost-reduction issues before them, the landscape has become littered with an alphabet soup of dueling cost-reduction methodologies. Total Quality Management (TQM), Just in Time (JIT), Overhead Budget Management (OBM), Total Quality Cost (TQC), and others all profess and, to varying degrees, provide useful responses to institutional concerns. However, underlying each of these methodologies is a concept that should resonate with all colleges and universities—quality. At every institution, student quality, faculty quality, teaching quality, and research quality are highly valued. Productivity may, in fact, be the wrong word to use regarding higher education. Instead of pursuing productivity, perhaps colleges and universities should pursue quality within realistic and appropriate financial parameters.

Many colleges and universities find themselves in the difficult position of trying to fund—with shrinking resources—the institutions they have become during the past forty years. For many, it will be impossible. Across-the-board budget cuts dilute the quality of existing programs and jeopardize the programs that aspire to greatness. In aggregate, higher education in the United States has reached a programmatic and cost size that can no longer be supported with available resources. As fewer and fewer resources are distributed across a broad programmatic base, institutions risk a slow deterioration in quality.

The pursuit of quality is not without peril, however. In Chapter 3, William Massy draws a very important distinction between design quality and implementation quality, using an analogy of BMWs and Fords. He argues that while a BMW may have more *design* quality than a Ford, the Ford is less expensive and can still meet the quality needs of its owner. The key is that design quality must be measured against the task at hand. A cruise missile is an extremely well designed weapon but is inappropriate for taking out a mosquito on the back patio. Implementation quality, on the other hand, addresses how well a product or service meets its design specifications. If a fly swatter is deemed to be the appropriate extermination device for the mosquito, then it should be a very good fly swatter. A high-quality implementation of the fly-swatter production process should produce excellent fly swatters at the lowest reasonable costs. The distinction between design quality and implementation quality is critical. The unbridled pursuit of design quality may well yield the academic version of the cruise missile/mosquito analogy. Programmatic design quality must be bounded by institutional needs and resources and implemented in a high-quality manner.

Toward Efficiency and Effectiveness

If quality is to be the driving force behind institutional change, then some important steps need to be taken.

1. Determine institutional financial equilibrium.

Each institution must realistically calculate how much money is available to be spent currently and for the future. While seemingly self-evident, this has not been the practice within higher education. The concept of financial equilibrium broadly examines an institution's financial structure, given its mission, to ensure its short- and long-term financial health. A balanced budget does not necessarily mean that an institution is in a state of financial equilibrium. If the endowment spending rate is too high and no funds are being reinvested in facilities, the long-range financial health of the institution is in jeopardy. The budget may be balanced, but at what future cost? The purchasing power of the endowment and the functional value of the facilities are eroding. Yet, this is the tactic many schools use to balance budgets. In essence, these institutions have been living beyond their means and have invaded their capital to do it.

In determining financial equilibrium, each college and university must ask and realistically answer several questions.

- What is the appropriate market-based tuition price that it can afford to charge? Historically, the industry has utilized a cost-plus pricing strategy: Here's how much we need to spend; let's set prices accordingly. Most institutions were able to get away with this approach during the robust economic growth of the 1980s. However, this model has systematically outstripped parental and student ability to pay the bill and led to ever-growing financial aid budgets (in the form of tuition discounts). In the early 1990s, many institutions were netting only 25 to 30 cents of each marginal dollar of increased tuition. A market-based pricing approach focuses less on what the institution needs and more on people's willingness and ability to pay.

- How much should be reinvested in the physical plant to maintain its functional value to the institution? American colleges and universities have accumulated a staggering $60-billion backlog of capital renewal and deferred maintenance. Programmatic growth and balanced budgets have been achieved, in part, at the expense of existing facilities.

- How much debt can the institution sustain?

- What endowment spending rate will preserve endowment purchasing power? A number of institutions have slowly increased spending rates as a short-term budget-balancing measure. However, this is a slippery slope for most institutions because it is very easy to become addicted to those revenues.

- What is a realistic level of sponsored research given the growing competition for those dollars?

- What is a reasonable enrollment level for the institution given our standards and demographics?

- How much money can we realistically expect to raise from our donor base?

The answers to these questions will vary from institution to institution. In the end, however, realistic answers will identify an institution's unique financial-equilibrium pressure points and determine how much money is available for programs and operations.

2. Determine what can be afforded.

Having determined the institution's points of financial equilibrium, faculty members and administrators must answer the fundamental question: What programs of appropriate quality can we afford? Answering it is not a simple undertaking. During the growth period of the past forty years, many institutions have attempted to be all things to all people. Programs have grown topsy-turvy at many institutions, largely in response to competitive pressures. However, as student demand abates and costs continue to rise, numerous colleges and universities can no longer maintain program quality. As one university president asked, "Am I better off with ten mediocre programs or five excellent programs?"

This concept of selective excellence will have to prevail throughout the industry if reasonable quality standards are to be maintained. Each institution will have to systematically address its programmatic strengths and weaknesses to identify what is worth keeping, what should be improved, and what should be discarded. Simply making the entire program base more productive is unrealistic and inappropriate. Traditional productivity concepts (i.e., more output, cost-benefit analysis, etc.) have limited value. Colleges and universities should have a solid understanding of their program revenues and costs. However, merely increasing class size and ballooning student-faculty ratios will only diminish quality. Costs may be controlled but it is to the long-run detriment of the institution and its students. Education is a labor-intensive and capital-intensive industry. Although technology may play a greater role in the delivery of educational services in the future, the basic educational exchange still takes place between good faculty and good students. The challenge for institutions is to determine which of those exchanges they can afford to do best, remembering that they cannot afford all of them.

Design quality should play an important role in shaping programs. What is in the best interest of students, faculty, and the institution? As Massy and Zemsky argue, faculty activity has moved away from institutional goals toward the activities that enhance a faculty member's standing within his or her discipline (research, publishing, etc.). Consequently, program design and infrastructure often reflect BMW design quality when a Ford or Chevy would be more appropriate (i.e., departments that offer a broad range of specialty courses but have few or no majors). The BMW design quality should not be arbitrarily dismissed, but it must be tempered by institutional resource constraints, other programmatic needs, and student needs.

3. Reconsider administrative activities.

In his chapter, Massy points to a number of factors that degrade the productivity of administrative functions—organizational slack and task accretion, to name a few. These problems, while not unique to higher education, are pervasive within it.

The basic challenge in this area is defining the outputs of administration. What exactly do administrators do? A scan at the typical institution will usually find people working hard. Paper is flowing. Approvals are granted. Reports are issued. Yet, is all of that work really needed? And if it is necessary, is it done efficiently and effectively?

Anecdotes about cumbersome administrative processes and bureaucratic snafus abound. At one institution, five approvals are required for a faculty member's change of address to be entered into the personnel information system. (Presumably, the faculty member would have to move back to his or her previous home if approval were denied!) At another, a labyrinthine purchasing process groans inexorably forward, turning tens of thousands of requisitions into tens of thousands of purchase orders. Throughout, stamps and signatures of approval are collected, adding mostly cost and little value to the transaction. In many ways, such administrative processes are control systems that happen to provide services to users rather than appropriately controlled service systems. Reorienting such processes around essential activities and focusing on customer service most often produces greater productivity and improved service quality. Administration should not be an end in itself.

To begin assessing administrative activities, each institution must answer several sets of questions.

- Does the institution need all of the administrative activities currently performed? What can be eliminated with no perceptible harm to the college? What is nice to do but not essential?
- What are the key processes through which work gets done? (Few administrative departments carry out work by themselves. Typically, most work processes involve multiple departments that are linked to

provide some service. Registration, purchasing, personnel, financial aid, and budgeting are good examples of multi-departmental processes.) How well designed are these processes? Does the work flow smoothly? How long does it take to get something done? How much does it cost to product the desired output? Are there needless and unnecessary steps involved? Does institutional decentralization produce redundancy and added cost in administrative activities? (Massy's chapter highlights a number of analytical approaches for evaluating process flow.)

- Can these work processes be redesigned from the bottom up? Most work processes typically start with noble goals—to better control and mobilize institutional purchasing power, to more effectively register students, or to more effectively produce payroll checks. Over time, however, layer upon layer of added tasks, steps, and controls are added to such processes. The end product of this evolved, rather than designed, approach is often a monster that devours its young. The process assumes a life of its own while its costs rise and the quality of its service declines. Pieces of the process are "owned" by individual departmental managers, but no one "owns" the overall process.

A more logically and rationally designed administrative infrastructure can yield lower costs overall and higher-quality service. Productivity becomes a by-product of good implementation quality, assuming the design quality is appropriate for the task at hand.

THE NEED FOR CHANGE AND LEADERSHIP

The preceding section speaks directly to the need for change in the way colleges and universities are managed. Much of the change is basic. It requires a rethinking of the financial management of the institution, a focus on academic quality in light of shrinking resources, and a reorienting of administrative efforts around essential tasks and activities. Yet, despite the seeming simplicity of the proposed changes, such undertakings are fraught with career-limiting implications for those initiating them. More than one job has been lost in challenging institutional culture and inertia.

The key to the basic change required in higher education is leadership. Without it, little can happen and institutional inertia will prevail. The exercise of strong leadership in higher education can be a Bermuda Triangle of sorts, a place where strange fates and disappearances occur. However, it is essential for effective change. Despite the cutting-edge thinking and research that takes place within colleges and universities, institutions themselves are not predisposed to change. And when change occurs, it happens very slowly. Although consensus management (where an 11-to-1 vote represents a tie) has many positive attributes, it does not foster the dramatic change required at many institutions. Certainly, institutional leaders must work with and through faculty members and staff, but bold initiatives are seldom born in committees.

An appropriate starting point may well be the notion of reinventing the institution. Most people are familiar with the concept of zero-based budgeting. Perhaps the concepts of zero-based operations needs to be invented. If an institution went out of business at 5 p.m. on a given day and started anew at 9 a.m. the next morning, would it do things the same way? Probably not. Certain programs would likely be jettisoned, administrative procedures simplified, and a tighter, higher-quality institution created. If all of this sounds a bit simplistic, it could well be. However, it is exactly the type of breakthrough thinking and return to basics so many schools need. The necessary changes will more likely occur if institutional leaders climb above the fray of institutional politics.

SUMMARY

The preceding discussion might appear to be more about strategy than about productivity and quality. However, it is important to recognize that productivity and quality have become strategic issues. Increased productivity is not a tactical response to a transient issue. It must become imbedded in institutional cultures for the long-term reasons of quality and robust survival. The primary challenge for all institutions is not downsizing but rightsizing. Each institution must be "sized" programmatically and administratively to fit its available resources given its mission and quality standards.

Business as usual is a highly risky mode of operation in this decade. Unless productivity is internalized and recognized as a strategic issue, colleges and universities may well be swept up in the tornado alluded to at the beginning of this paper. Dorothy and Toto were also consumed by a Kansas whirlwind and embarked on an odyssey in search of home and the gentle Auntie Em. Institutions that continue to search for the comforts of their "home" of the past forty years may be in for a rude awakening. When they get there, they may well find that Auntie Em has moved.

Chapter 1

Productivity and the Academic "Business"

Stephen Joel Trachtenberg
President
George Washington University

It is generally agreed that something must be done to improve the productivity of our institutions of higher education. Yet when it comes to discussing the subject, instructors and administrators can be extremely sensitive. In this amusing parable, Stephen Joel Trachtenberg explores the reactions people have to the very mention of the topic and shows that, after many years, there are still those who think of "productivity" and "higher education" as mutually exclusive terms.

Never has productivity in higher education been more important than today, as we move relentlessly toward the twenty-first century. Bringing more revenue into their budgets without adding unnecessarily to expenditures is what every American college and university is currently struggling to accomplish.

It is this concern for revenues as much as the "pure" concern for undergraduate education that is driving the new calls for a better balance between the teaching and research commitments of our academic institutions. Increasingly, university administrators have had to face the fact that while undergraduate tuition provides a vital portion of the money that they spend on personnel and facilities, undergraduates do not always directly benefit from those expenditures. To what extent this reapportioning of funds hurts undergraduate opportunities is being watched more closely and controlled more carefully by responsible academic institutions, although many schools continue to be possessed by the faculty-researcher star syndrome.

Such being the case, we need to confront the fact that the title of this chapter will undoubtedly stir up furious resentment in the hearts of most professors and quite a number of administrators—as illustrated by the entirely fictional parable that follows, whose invented characters should not be confused with any actual human beings, alive or dead.

THE PARABLE: BACK TO PAST VIRTUES, HOME AGAIN TO OUR FUTURE IMPERFECT

Once I had decided to compose this chapter, I asked the physics department and the engineering school of my university to create a time-travel machine for me. They came through in record time, and, with the help of our law school, the gadget was quickly patented. Our business school was soon negotiating the machine's sale to a Japanese company that promised to build its primary plant on our new campus in northern Virginia.

It was just a few weeks before beginning the first draft that I clambered into this remarkable machine, not without some trepidation, and made my voyage back to 1959, when I was a senior at the undergraduate men's college of Columbia University.

It was as if I had never left. Indeed, I kept expecting to run into myself, rushing across the quad on the way to a class in Hamilton Hall. Instead, I literally bumped into the president of the university, who was making his way across the campus at his usual stately pace, homburg firmly in place, herringbone tweed coat impeccably fitted, his gray mustache neatly trimmed.

"I beg your pardon, Mr. President," I exclaimed, "but you happen to be exactly the person I'm looking for. Could I ask you for a moment of your time? Perhaps we could sit on that bench just behind you? There is a question that I seriously need to ask."

He looked skeptical, and I heard a low guttural sound come from the depths of the herringbone tweed—but he did sit down. I launched into the following disquisition:

"Mr. President, I know this will seem a bit unbelievable, but you've probably noticed by now that I bear an eerie middle-aged resemblance to one of the seniors currently attending the college—an energetic and rather involved young man named Stephen Joel Trachtenberg. No, I'm not his father or his uncle. I am *he himself.* And I've come here all the way from the early 1990s—when I am a university president too—to ask you how you feel about the subject of productivity and the academic business."

The president looked a bit doubtful as I described my trip from the future, but his face didn't settle into a mask of complete disbelief until he heard those last words.

"Young man," he began—because in those days you were considered a young man, probably quite rash and feckless, until you were on the verge of 60—"young man, I congratulate you on your vivid imagination, as well as your remarkable resemblance to the student you mentioned. Next time, however, make certain that you don't venture too far from the realm of plausibility. Serious academic study will never be a *business,* as you so laughably suggest. And as for *productivity*—if I heard you correctly—I suppose that has something to do with factories that make things, such as automobiles and refrigerators, and therefore cannot be applied to the purposes and ideals of our universities as those institutions have grown and developed over a period of nearly 1,000 years."

Without pausing for further comment, he majestically rose until his gray coat hung straight from his broad shoulders, adjusted his homburg, and marched off in the direction of Lowe Library. Meanwhile, the beeper in my own coat pocket was urgently summoning me for the return trip to my own time. I pushed my way through the gaggle of students and security guards surrounding my time machine, which was parked illegally in front of Hartley Hall, and made my way back to the future, or rather, the present.

When I reached my campus, feeling only a little bit the worse for wear, I was greeted by an unofficial delegation of five colleagues who announced that they had urgent business with me.

"President Trachtenberg," said the first colleague, "I'm sorry to inform you that we are very upset by the essay we understand you are composing on the subject of productivity and the academic business. Frankly, we regard the subject as the absolute nadir of some of the worst trends we've seen developing in the academic world in the past ten years. We're profoundly disturbed that it should be the president of our own university who is making such a spectacle of himself!"

"Spectacle?" I retorted. "Is it a spectacle to join a group of distinguished authorities like my fellow authors, all of whom agree that even not-for-profit institutions require actual money to pay salaries and fringe benefits—not to mention building maintenance, landscaping, library acquisitions, student services, admissions work, financial aid programs, laboratory supplies, and data processing equipment?"

"You don't understand," observed colleague number two with a faint smile. "That's what the administration is there for. It's *your* function to raise the money, and it's the role of faculty governance to make the decisions on how it ought to be spent. We're the ones on the academic front lines. We're the ones who understand, better than anyone else possibly can, the needs posed by our professional commitments to our students. For you to refer to productivity and to the academic business . . . well, that implies quite a different kind of metaphor, one drawn from the *corporate* sector of the economy where altogether different rules apply."

"Exactly right," agreed colleague number three. "And I must say, President Trachtenberg, that we're inclined to regard talk like that as being equivalent to a counterrevolution against the hard-won rights and privileges of the American professoriate. My own field being political science, I'm inclined to conclude that you'd like very much to be in the position of a traditional boss, who would like to extract productivity from the hands on his assembly line."

"Absolutely!" exclaimed colleague number four. "All of us know that where higher education is concerned, definitions of productivity are entirely subjective—except by the grossest of financial measures. Do you mean *teaching* productivity in terms of hours spent in the classroom or the number of students taught? Do you mean teaching productivity in terms of quality? And if so, quality as defined by whom? Or do you mean teaching productivity in terms of the long-term benefits actually received by students—and how would you go about measuring that, given the fact that individuals might benefit from higher education in different ways at different points in their lives, all the way through to their senior-citizen years?

"Perhaps you mean *research* productivity? How would you go about measuring that? It took me twelve years to complete my absolutely definitive monograph on an obscure but highly influential poet of the sixteenth century. In those twelve years I published not a single article or book review! Should I be considered less productive than someone from another discipline who, in the same space of time, published twenty articles or three books?

"And if by any chance you mean *financial* productivity—the ability of professors to attract, as you call it, business and to maximize the pay-off on the hours they invest in the classroom or laboratory—would you explain to us how such a system could favor anyone who isn't a wildly popular teacher with huge lecture classes or a superman-level researcher who pulls in massive government funds or foundation grants?"

"My friends," I finally managed to say, "aren't you overreacting to what is, after all, just the title of a chapter in a book? The fact is that most of the book won't even address academic matters but will be concerned with things like financial management, intellectual property, facilities management, and—"

"Hogwash!" Colleague number five could no longer contain herself. "You aren't dealing with illiterates, you know. You're dealing with Ph.D.'s who can spot the thin edge of a wedge when they see it. Don't think we missed the article in the *Chronicle of Higher Education* that described how English universities are terminating professors for financial reasons. They can't attract enough students to cover their own paychecks and fringe benefits—meaning, presumably, that they're insufficiently *productive.* They've already let a professor of philosophy go. Next to be deemed unprofitable—thrown out on their ears at the age of 40 or 50—will be those working on the 'wrong' languages or literatures, the ones working in anthropology rather than computer science, and, of course, the ones working in pure science rather than business or applied technology.

"As far as we can see, President Trachtenberg," she continued, "by even contributing to a book like this one you're practically opening the door to and helping to create the climate for similar moves in *this* country!"

And there we stood, looking at one another across a gap as wide as the Grand Canyon.

"Colleagues," I uttered in a slightly quavering voice, "forgive me for getting personal, but do you have *any* idea how hard we have to run in order to stay, financially, in the same place? At the beginning of this year our costs for major medical insurance went up 94 percent. As of right now, the hard work we're doing to attract better students has involved massive increases in scholarship aid. And at a time when the most elite universities and colleges have moved well over the $20,000 mark for a single year's tuition, we've been hearing discussions—and complaints—about productivity and academia from a number of sources."

Thirty seconds of silence ticked by, broken finally by the political scientist. "You're trying to panic us," he snapped, "and it's not going to work. Your methodology is entirely unsound. I haven't heard a single relevant fact or piece of solidly grounded data in what you've been saying since this discussion began. President Trachtenberg, do we have any hope of convincing you to call the editors and tell them that a severe case of writer's block has led your personal physician to recommend half a year of complete literary abstinence?"

I thought that over, and replied, "Not really, I'm afraid. But having reflected on how concerned you are about these matters, I can promise you that I will think about adding the following subtitle: *The Single Most Urgent and Possibly Insoluble Problem Confronting Higher Education in a Period of Escalating Costs, Escalating Tuition, and Growing Disenchantment Among Average Americans, Corporate Leaders, and Legislators with the Academic Enterprise As It Is Presently Defined and Conducted in the United States.*

"It does give the essay a distinctly more academic ring, doesn't it?" I remarked as I turned to the technicians and ordered them to destroy the time-travel machine as quickly as possible. I then left the group and headed straight to my office to tell our business dean that the machine was no longer for sale. The last thing I wanted to inflict on higher education was a heightened and possibly despair-inducing realization that the vision of academic life shared by most academicians has changed very little since the late 1950s while the world around us has changed, is changing, and looks as if it will continue to change a very great deal indeed.

THE REALITY: HIGHER EDUCATION IN STEP WITH THE WORLD AT LARGE

"The day is long past when any university's faculty members, administrators, or staff can take its elegant seals, ceremonies, maces, and robes as a kind of divine guarantee that the payroll will always be met and life will always remain magically stable. Even the strongest Fortune 500 companies, which have capitalization sufficient to carry them through several very lean years, are currently looking at their budgets—right down to the most trivial but collectively huge expenditures—with eagle eyes and trembling hearts.

This is not a parable. The fiscal future of the entire United States is currently in question. Contrary prophecies and scenarios regarding that future long ago leaped from the pages of major business journals and newspaper and news magazine business sections into the daily parlance of the American people. In a world of this kind, it must be clearly understood that independent institutions of higher education are 'independent' only insofar as they cannot, at present, be *directly* told what to do by government agencies. But as long as independent schools exist by the acts of sufferance known as governmental charters, even that could change if our national and international economic situation becomes sufficiently serious. It behooves us all to think and act accordingly. Every person on a university's payroll, as well as alumni and friends, must introduce a strong component of responsible fiscal thinking into their efforts on behalf of that university.

And please note that I have not once used the word *productivity* in this conclusion. What's the sense in bringing up such a volatile word when the real need it represents is having a hard enough time on its own?

Chapter 2

The Constraints on Campus Productivity

Robert Birnbaum

Professor, Higher Education
Center for Higher Education, Governance,
and Leadership
University of Maryland College Park

Two customary measures of productivity are the efficiency of a process and its ultimate effectiveness. At institutions of higher education, productivity is a complex combination of both, yet getting different campus constituencies to agree on what exactly is meant by "efficient" and "effective" is nearly impossible. Robert Birnbaum examines four points of view frequently encountered among campus leaders faced with the challenge of improving productivity and discusses some generalizations that can be drawn from them.

"I have no doubt that in something as loose as a university there will be unproductive elements. But if you tighten it to, say, an IBM, you would destroy it—destroy its spontaneity, creativity, and freedom. It's easy to say that institutions are not productive, but compared to what?"

"Years ago I felt that we should hold institutions responsible—if we get X money we should graduate Y students. But now I realize that you can't have a rigid formula. It's not a production line."

"The simple-minded approach [to productivity] is to ask professors to teach more classes. . . . It's not as simple as businessmen think it is. Bennett gave the academy a bum rap on productivity."

The statements above were not made by self-serving professors or by defensive administrators but by institutional trustees with high-level experience in the corporate and government sectors. These comments illustrate the difficulty that even accomplished individuals have in trying to understand or manage productivity in an academic environment. Colleges and universities are not neatly configured, button-down organizations, and there is no single formula that can be plugged in across the broad spectrum of higher education to raise productivity levels. Improving academic productivity will require understanding colleges and universities from multiple perspectives.

This chapter attempts to clarify the issue of increasing productivity in higher education in light of the rational, cultural, political, and cognitive constraints that currently define its reality. The information presented is based on intensive interviews with seventy trustees, administrators, and faculty leaders at seven institutions that reflect the diversity that exists in higher education today—two universities, two state colleges, two private colleges, and one community college. Their enrollment ranged from less than 1,000 to more than 40,000 and their expenditure per student ranged from $2500 to $21,000.

DEFINING PRODUCTIVITY

Productivity is a ratio between inputs and outputs. Productivity improves when increases of output are achieved per unit of input. This definition fits well when applied to limited mechanical processes, but when applied to complex human activities—particularly education—the meaning becomes obscured.

In higher education, productivity is not simply effectiveness; any institution can become more effective if it need not limit costs. And it is not only efficiency, since the quantity of outputs can be maintained at lower cost if quality is not a concern. Productivity is the combination of both concepts into a multidomain construct.

There are two major aspects to understanding the concept of productivity in higher education. The first is political. The selection, interpretation, importance, and measurement of input and output variables in a productivity calculation are subject to differing interpretations based on the values of the observer. For instance, higher education has many purposes, of which enrolling students, awarding credits, and producing graduates are only the most obvious. The different constituents of an institution, such as students, administrators, alumni, parents, legislators, faculty, suppliers, and local community inhabitants, are likely to have different ideas about what it is supposed to be doing. Being more productive on a dimension considered desirable by one constituency may often make the institution less productive on a dimension valued by another. The calculation of productivity is therefore an inherently political act. The measurement must be made from the vantage point of a single group and almost certainly will not give full consideration to the inputs or outputs perceived as important by other legitimate groups. If there is no agreement on inputs and outputs, by definition there can be no agreement on the measurement of productivity.

The second aspect is cognitive. The number of variables involved in determining productivity is so large and the interactions between them so uncertain that calculating total-factor productivity—the efficiency of transforming all inputs into a combination of all outputs—is not merely difficult but impossible. There are many reasons for this, but perhaps the essence is captured best in the charming aphorism that education is a process of "converting tangible resources into intangible resources," found in *Productivity: Burden of Success.* A literal interpretation of this truism is that colleges and universities are in the business of transforming things that are measurable into things that are not. For example, in *The Costs of Higher Education,* Bowen defines the product of higher education as "learning in all its manifestations, [which] consists primarily of changes in people—changes in their knowledge, their characteristics, and their behavior." The goal of higher education, he writes, is to help set people "on a course of continuing and desirable activity and, through them, to achieve broad social and cultural advancement of the entire society."

But there is no consensus on what any of these variables mean and no algorithm that suggests how they can be measured or related to inputs. In an attempt to simplify the measurement of productivity, Mahoney writes in *Productivity Defined: The Relativity of Efficiency, Effectiveness, and Change,* that groups must rely on partial-factor productivity definitions that may often relate selected output variables to a single input factor. However, while such calculations are not necessarily wrong, they are, of necessity, incomplete. People interviewed for this chapter thought of inputs not only in terms of money and other tangible resources but also in terms of students, organizations, programs, and individual efforts. They also differed about the degree to which outputs should be considered as they related to students and learning, to scholarship and research, and to the effects on society as a whole.

It is essential to realize that when defining productivity in higher education, the selection of input and output variables is arbitrary and based on personal values and social consensus rather than on a rational understanding of organizational or system processes. Productivity in higher education is as difficult to quantify as it is to manage.

The various views of inputs and outputs proposed by respondents in this study indicate some of the problems inherent in the concept of productivity. These difficulties would have been multiplied had the views of other campus-involved groups been included. However, even the admittedly limited perspectives that comprise this chapter permit the following generalizations to be made.

Measuring Productivity

The research reported in this chapter indicates that there were at least two major ways to measure productivity—one emphasized efficiency and the other, quality. Efficiency and quality were frequently seen as inherently in conflict. As one administrator said, "I was raised to believe that you get what you pay for, and less cost may not be efficient. If we push efficiency, we may lose quality, for example, by increasing the number of courses taught by part-time faculty." And quality was also seen to be partially in conflict with itself. For example, improving quality by improving undergraduate instruction could require additional demands on faculty time, delivery systems, and administrative support systems and therefore hinder improvements in research. As Cameron has noted, because of cognitive and resource limitations, it is impossible for an institution to simultaneously maximize all dimensions of quality.

While most respondents in the study agreed that increases in productivity would be desirable, in the absence of accepted definitions or indicators, nothing could be done that would satisfy every constituency. Institutions were caught in catch-22 situations. If, for example, administrators committed resources to collect and analyze the additional data that were presumed by one interest group to drive productivity, they were likely, as a consequence, to be attacked by another group for misplaced priorities. Sometimes these opposing pressures came from different voices in a single constituency; sometimes they even came from the same voice! The problem was that those who clamored for productivity and accountability didn't know what they wanted, couldn't accept the logic of trade-offs, couldn't decide how much of anything was enough, and couldn't agree on how much progress had been made. There was, therefore, no way that any level of campus performance could be judged as satisfactory.

Most respondents seemed unaware that productivity involved both joint costs and joint products. Any approach to measuring productivity that suggested a direct input/output linearity oversimplified and distorted what was in fact a nonlinear process. This complexity made it impossible to understand what elements of an existing program directly affected productivity and what the consequences of any proposed changes might be.

The Trade-offs

While institutions were under pressure to optimize each of the factors that contribute to increased productivity, the reality was that trade-offs had to be made. The bare fact was stated by an administrator: "If we want research and scholarship and public service, inevitably that means less time spent in classrooms." Although respondents at some institutions claimed that research strengthened teaching, many others recognized that increased attention to research detracted from teaching and reduced the time professors spent with students.

Trade-offs also occurred between quality and efficiency. The on-campus perspective was that the achievement of quality requires inefficiency. Individuals at comparatively prosperous campuses were as likely as those at less affluent ones to believe that quality required reduced class sizes, smaller teaching loads, and more full-time faculty—all of which would increase costs. An administrator with a background in finance and education summed up the dilemma: "From the business point of view, [productivity] means credit hours per [full-time equivalent] faculty—the more credit hours, the more productivity. From [the education] perspective, productivity [is] an unquantifiable measure of students going through the system—what the system has contributed to their life. It's nice when the two come together, but it doesn't often happen."

Assessing Productivity

A few respondents refused to even consider productivity as a reasonable concept to apply to colleges and universities. These individuals believed that anyone who even raised the issue was not grounded in a clear sense of what goes on at an academic institution. But most believed that the concept, while problematic, was legitimate, and they were not necessarily opposed to measuring productivity.

The problem in assessing productivity was that the elements that could be directly measured were acknowledged as being not very important, and important elements that could be identified in general could not be measured in any valid or reliable way. Many respondents agreed with a board member who said that one could judge productivity by looking at the product—"the difference the college makes to the students who graduate from it each year." They assumed that because students had apparently been successful, their institutions were therefore productive. These respondents were likewise convinced that students who were satisfied with their education or who had successful careers provided prima facie evidence of productivity; they did not consider whether the same result could have been achieved at lower cost or whether anything different might have become of those students had they attended different institutions.

In general, most respondents thought that over the two-year period of this study quality and efficiency had improved (or at least had not diminished) at their respective institutions. At the same time, some respondents on every campus and every respondent on some campuses agreed that further improvements in quality and efficiency would also improve productivity. Yet there were few campuses where improved productivity was a major institutional priority.

THE CONSTRAINTS ON PRODUCTIVITY

There were a number of reasons why campus leaders found it difficult to increase productivity more than they believed they already had. These reasons can be categorized according to the different ways that organizations are viewed—perspectives that suggest particular managerial orientations. Let us consider the constraints on productivity as seen from the rational, cultural, political, and cognitive perspectives. Collectively, these perspectives illustrate the complexity of the issue and present a more accurate understanding of why increasing productivity in higher education has proved to be so difficult.

The Rational Perspective

Many respondents were, in part, managers (trustees, administrators, or faculty whose interactions and perceptions have an effect on institutional productivity) with a rational orientation who believed that improved productivity could be accomplished by relating means to ends and calculating costs and benefits. What follows are the constraints these people saw as they surveyed opportunities for increased productivity at their institutions.

Structure. Several obvious constraints are built into the structure of higher education and are part of the givens with which rational managers must contend. One of the most rigid limitations is the labor intensiveness of higher education, which has led to cost increases that have exceeded general economic inflation. These increases, which have been documented over the past sixty years by June O'Neill and others, suggest that the difficulties of increasing productivity may not be so much a defect in administrative will as a consequence of a basic characteristic of higher education as an industry.

A second structural constraint was inherent in the organizational and decision-making configuration of the institutions themselves. The nature of academic institutions—the unusual degree of decentralization and the principle of faculty autonomy in certain critical areas—made administration-driven productivity changes difficult to plan, implement, or control. As one administrator noted, these institutional peculiarities "lead to the inability to say 'improve productivity' and see it happen instantly. Sometimes little things occur that shouldn't. People should fix things, but don't. Sometimes it's difficult to get things done."

A third structural constraint to productivity, and probably the one most noted by the public, was higher education's traditional antipathy to management and efficiency. Respondents agreed that on many campuses productivity was inhibited by managerial inefficiency due to low morale, incompetence, and lethargy. Faculty who had "retired on the job" and were not fulfilling their responsibilities also had an impact on productivity.

But the rational manager, while clearly understanding these problems, also understood the difficulties of trying to correct them and often accurately believed that attempts at remediation would probably make things worse rather than better.

Resources. Productivity often requires investment, and, while some institutions have the resources that allow them to make such investments, many do not. Money is needed for microcomputers, instructional equipment, additional instructional space, updated facilities, and support personnel (e.g., additional secretaries to free faculty of clerical duties and permit them to make better use of their time). But on many campuses even minimal financial support was hard to come by. A trustee who was a corporate CEO said, "The fundamental thing to improve efficiency is to have more financial resources. It's always hand to mouth. With more facilities and dollars, we could get more from the faculty and operate more efficiently."

The lack of resources not only made it difficult to implement programs that could improve productivity by managing people and space better, but also prevented administrators from staying ahead of the game by not allowing them time to set agendas, to put proposals on the table, and to set the parameters of discussion.

The other resource constraint identified was not fiscal but intellectual. At some institutions, faculty appointed in the past on the criteria of that time were not able to respond to new institutional programs and missions. On other campuses, intellectual constraints were attributed to administrators. At many institutions, planning and analytic techniques proposed to increase productivity often required more training and experience than administrators commonly had.

Data. At some campuses there were few data related to productivity. In many cases, people were often unaware of what data were available and those data could often be equivocal—offering little assistance in assessing productivity. Substantial financial resources appeared to be a necessary requirement for adequate data, but that alone did not ensure its availability. Some institutions had extensive resources, but their history and traditions did not support data-related decision making.

One administrator, noting that demands for accountability were often not matched with the fiscal support that might make it possible, said, "If we had more data on lots of things we could be more efficient and effective. We need more research support, administrative support. What's preventing us from doing these things is . . . funding. The weak infrastructure has really put us so far out of kilter that . . . reallocation can't do it. But infrastructure problems are not very sexy; it's hard to get funds for it."

Costs and Benefits. The rational manager knew that it was easy, conceptually, to design programs that would increase productivity but that for many reasons the actual outcomes could be quite different than those expected. Because experience suggested that time spent on improving productivity might not be cost effective, the rational manager was cautious about implementing new programs. For example, if a productivity program that required major expenditures of time and energy resulted in only marginal changes in output or had unanticipated or negative consequences, it would actually be unproductive. Changes were easier to make in nonacademic areas, but at many institutions even those opportunities were limited because nonacademic activities were underfunded to begin with.

At some institutions there was often no advantage for one subunit to make productivity changes because the benefits would often accrue to another. At public institutions, savings generated by productivity measures could not only be forfeit to the state but could in fact cause them to be penalized. An administrator described how the system worked: "We try to hold back positions in case we get in budget trouble. The state says that if you don't fill all your positions, that's proof you don't need them. They won't let us hoard our resources and be good managers."

Administrative Regulations. Administrative regulations and standard operating procedures were developed by institutions or imposed on them for purposes of efficiency and accountability. However, rational managers often found these regulations and procedures to hinder productivity. This was seen most frequently among public institutions. Resources were often allocated to campuses by fund categories (or even smaller budget subdivisions) and were not fungible. Savings in one fund could not be used in another, which sometimes led managers into nonproductive, but rationally necessary, left-hand, right-hand paradoxes. At one campus, for example, a lack of curbing caused lawns to be rutted by truck tires and to require continuous maintenance that, over time, cost more than curbs would to construct. But while lawn maintenance was funded from the operating budget, which the managers could adjust, curb construction required capital funds, over which managers had no control.

In addition, all institutions were bound by contractual arrangements with employees and contractors, and some were bound by the requirements of external agencies. Under these circumstances, the idea of increasing productivity could strike them as absurd. As one administrator said, "I don't know what productivity is. I have a locked-up labor force with thousands of regulations about what they can do. They are employed for life. I have a huge fixed cost, and a small variable cost. Where's my flexibility? The fabric is not designed for efficiency—it's designed to prevent discrimination. There's no consequence now for not doing a job, and no reward for a job done brilliantly."

Wages and Personnel. Salary levels, particularly in service areas such as data processing and maintenance, were often so low that institutions could not hire the best-qualified personnel. The short-term savings effected by low salaries were believed by some to be offset by diminished productivity in the long run. One administrator pointed out, "I could improve efficiency if I could hire better people. If I could pay more, they would pay for themselves. The costs of retraining and temps is enormous. My new people have no knowledge or experience, and reducing turnover at the margin makes a big difference. I can't even hire secretaries for researchers—they can't type or do anything—the faculty get angry and have to do it themselves."

In addition, a lack of support personnel reduced productivity by substituting the time of relatively low-paid clerical and administrative staff with the time of relatively high-paid professionals and by increasing the frustration level of other campus professionals.

Tenure. The rational manager was aware that the largest proportion of most budgets went to salaries, the largest proportion of salaries went to faculty, and the largest proportion of faculty was tenured. Tenure itself was not a hindrance to productivity, but there were tenured faculty who were unproductive and productivity improvements would require working with all faculty members. A faculty member acknowledged that "the biggest problem of productivity is what to do with the unproductive faculty." A trustee recognized a problem in merely assessing tenured faculty: "The college could be even more efficient if it could hold teachers accountable. If we could review a tenured teacher, maybe efficiency would increase. But evaluation of teaching is a threat. It can't be instituted directly. There would be a revolt." Some respondents went further and talked about improving productivity by removing tenured faculty in areas of low enrollment. But in the final analysis, as one administrator said, "There's not enough pressure to justify cutting tenured faculty, and the nontenured are often teaching in areas you can't do without."

The rational manager realized that less-productive tenured faculty were a cost of doing business, in part a trade-off for low academic salaries, about which little could be done. A trustee defined it clearly: "The problem here is an older faculty; there's no place for people to go as the college changes. There are historical inefficiencies caused by the age and mix of faculty. I can't do anything about it, so I don't worry about it. We'll grow our way out of it. There are the same problems in all kinds of businesses."

The Cultural Perspective

In *Organizational Culture in the Study of Higher Education,* Masland writes that the culture of an academic organization "induces purpose, commitment, and order; provides meaning and social cohesion; and clarifies and explains behavioral expectations." While the rational view sees a world of means and ends and costs and benefits, the cultural view sees a world of shared values, ideals, and beliefs through which an organization's participants decide what is real and what is important. In this chapter, the cultural view includes elements drawn from the generic values of higher education and from the experiences of individual institutions. What follows are the constraints to productivity as seen from that perspective.

Academic Culture. The concept of productivity that was developed in business and industrial organizations has never been accepted as a core value in higher education. Board members, with positions in the business community, and administrators, who regularly interact with government bureaus and other external groups, may have seen some merit in thinking about productivity as a value, but the notion was foreign to those who did the work of the campus—the faculty. As one faculty member protested, "The idea of productivity is used to count beans—people who [graduate]. The faculty don't think much about productivity—only administrators do."

Any college president who embraced ideas such as productivity—and attempted to implement them—was likely to face faculty displeasure at having violated accepted academic norms. According to Bensimon in *Viewing the Presidency: Perceptual Congruence Between Presidents and Leaders on Their Campuses,* such displeasure could weaken the president's ability to provide other forms of academic and symbolic leadership and, as a result, lessen his or her influence.

Unlike organizations in which the activities of workers are controlled through administration-driven initiatives, in higher education faculty expect to have a significant voice in the governance and management of the enterprise. The academic culture believes not only that administrative initiatives to improve productivity are improper but also that they are counter-productive. In that view, institutions are productive not despite the cultural constraints on administrative leadership but because of them. As one faculty member said, "One of the reasons we're so efficient is because decision-making is by the people who are the producers [the faculty] in shared decision-making. Being more collegial has made us more efficient and leads to better decisions."

Institutional Culture. In addition to the effects of academic culture in general, productivity was also interpreted through the particular circumstances and experiences of the individual institutions. Because of their intimate familiarity with campus life, respondents realized the difficulty of changing even situations known to be deficient. As one trustee said, "Efficiency here could be improved, but I'm not dissatisfied. I'm not sure we need some of the people we have in places they are now. But doing something about it is hard because of tradition, personal relationships, political situations."

The amount of resources appeared unrelated to concern for productivity, although poor and rich institutions had quite different reasons for explaining their lack of productivity motivation. Institutions with small resource bases had developed shared myths about their unusual achievements in the face of financial adversity and administrators believed they were already operating at maximum efficiency. Institutions with comparatively large resource bases had a different explanation. For them, comparatively low student-faculty ratios, proliferation of specialized courses, and lavish support of programs and activities related to the quality of student life were embedded in tradition. These elements certified their uniqueness and defined the meaning of the institution itself. To question existing programs and relationships—to even consider them in terms of costs and benefits—was to attack the core of the institution.

At some campuses, institutional size influenced the way people interacted and, therefore, affected productivity. Productivity was seen by some as having been diminished in institutions so large, complex, and impersonal that coordination was increasingly difficult. Productivity was hindered for different reasons at small and unitary institutions that had an aura of family. In a family-like culture, attempts to increase productivity could be seen as violating social norms. An administrator at one such institution said, "There's a 'nice guy' syndrome here. If you don't have high expectations and enforce them, you get mediocre performance. Here it's like a family." At another small campus, incompetence at all levels was tolerated to avoid confrontation, and continued employment was an expectation regardless of performance. Administrators challenged these assumptions at their own risk.

At some campuses, past experiences had created attitudes that were difficult to change. At one college, an administrator pointed out that the lack of cooperation between departments "has a lot to do with history. There are people in place at the college, they've been there a long time, they exert extraordinary control over outcomes. They don't have high positions—they've just managed to carve out a domain. . . . These same people have operated this way over three presidents."

The Political Perspective

Public discussions of institutional productivity often appear to assume that colleges are free agents—able to make independent decisions, to be internally cohesive, and to be responsive to the will of their formal leaders.

The political manager, however, was aware that at almost all institutions, some of these assumptions were not true, and that at some institutions, none of them were. Institutions were often subject to external forces beyond the control of their administrators, that made productivity gains difficult to achieve. Inside institutions, members of different subgroups had interests and preferences that conflicted as often as they converged. And while some formal leaders were strong enough to get their way most of the time, they never could do so all the time. In sum, political constraints on productivity came from outside the institution, from competing forces within it, and from the limited power of its formal leadership.

External Influences. All institutions depended on the external environment for their inputs and therefore, to some extent, were subject to forces over which they had little control. Although this was true for public and private institutions, colleges in the public sector appeared to be particularly vulnerable.

Probably the most significant external threat to productivity in the public sector came from the instability of financial resources. Several institutions in this study were subject to budget formulas that changed yearly or to budget-reduction orders that came midyear, after personnel commitments were made.

Even when finances could be guaranteed, there were other external policies that inhibited improvements in productivity at public institutions. For example, the carry-forward of unexpended budget balances could be limited, public funds might not be allocated to meet the obligations incurred by state negotiators in collective bargaining agreements, and colleges with enrollment-driven funding could be placed under enrollment caps that prevent them from generating increased revenues. Administrators could also find their institution boxed in by regulations applied uniformly to all government agencies, regardless of program or special needs, in the areas of purchasing, personnel, and construction, among others.

Some of the external pressures on public and private colleges were seen as related to the different roles played by their trustees. One administrator at a public university commented that "board members see themselves as the public watchdogs and not as protectors or friends of the campus like in the private sector." Once public agencies got into the productivity act, they could be as relentless as they were mindless. Administrators at an institution that had just undergone an external review that found "no evidence of systematic or widespread inefficiency" were nevertheless asked to "take additional steps to achieve greater efficiencies" on the grounds that any in-stitution with a budget its size should be able to do so.

At public colleges, mandates from trustees or other external groups usu-ally resulted in either rote compliance or covert subversion. The consequent paperwork not only diverted time, energy, and money from other activities but also discouraged campus officials and distracted them from what they felt was important.

Internal Competition. On many campuses, espoused goals and missions enjoyed wide campus support, but this masked real and significant differ-ences in the preferences of important campus subgroups. The reality at many institutions was that it was easy to produce a general statement of goals that everyone agreed upon, but that such statements were of little value because once they started to get specific, there were many disagree-ments. Resource allocation decisions were likely to be the result of negotia-tion, coalition formation, and compromise—influenced by everyone but ef-fectively controlled by no one.

Internal conflicts were apparent in the different interests of faculty and administration as well as among the faculty itself. Departments competed with each other for resources, hoarded what they had, and tried to get as much as they could. Productivity as a concept was not seen as being in the interest of the individual departments. As one trustee said, "No one likes to cut back from doing too much. There are vested interests at stake; there are opinions for what is appropriate in a discipline."

The political aspects of decision making with regard to productivity were most obvious to newly appointed administrators. Upon arriving at their re-spective campuses, they were struck by the less productive aspects of their systems. But as they gained experience and understood the expectations of the participants, they were likely to reduce their own aspirations. The politi-cal manager realized that many of the apparent opportunities for improved productivity were in fact the result of agreements or trade-offs made to gain specific advantages at some earlier time. In such cases, taking action to im-prove productivity would violate tacit agreements and reduce the adminis-trator's future ability to use political processes to achieve important objec-tives.

Campus Leaders. Campus leaders were limited in their ability to affect productivity for many reasons. Sometimes, as one trustee said, it was be-cause of lack of knowledge. Board members also found their involvement constrained by history or by conflicting forces. One trustee, who was a high-level corporate executive, thought that productivity improvements could be made in the area of faculty and curricula but believed that trustees could not get involved because the institution had a long history of delegation in those areas. On boards whose members took the view that they were like a corporate board of directors with the right to get involved in any operational aspects they desired, trustee involvement in academic issues drew backlashes from faculty and administrators.

Administrators also found themselves held back. Although a wide range of administrative options for improving productivity might appear possible, they saw that many options would ultimately have negative consequences. For example, an administrator pointed out that while workloads could be modified to make departments more productive, "If the department didn't agree, it would be difficult [for me] to influence course offerings. I can withhold staff, but it never goes over well. [I'm] seen as meddling in the department."

The political nature of campuses meant that improving productivity by directives simply did not work. Productivity had no internal political constituency and was no one's priority. Leaders could not use the concept as a rallying cry to which followers would respond. As one administrator put it, productivity is "as much a political as an academic issue. I used to develop ratios and stuff— student/faculty, class size—but no one was interested in them. Our greatest interest is in looking at quality, not efficiency. Our concerns revolve around the need to gain consensus through political means, and get people to buy in. You can't employ Tayloristic, top-down, rationalistic approaches. People have to be induced. It may require patronage or bribery, and it precludes being too tight-assed about efficiency."

From the political perspective, many ideas about how to increase productivity often ignored internal and external politics and the problems of resource acquisition and utilization that characterize the complexities of the real world.

The Cognitive Perspective

The rational, cultural, and political perspectives reported in the preceding sections were presented using composite statements in which respondents consciously reflected on their experiences related to productivity. The fourth model, the cognitive perspective, is presented quite differently. While it draws upon respondent statements, it emphasizes not their conscious reflections but rather how their perceptions may have been filtered, altered, or biased by constraints of which they were unaware.

Learning. The inputs and outputs that define productivity are difficult to measure, and the causal relationships between them in academic settings are largely unknown. In an effort to bring order from ambiguity, campus participants may construct elaborate scenarios of cause and effect (which they will also use to explain future events). In the absence of objective criteria, what they learn from these scenarios often may be incorrect. There are many sources for such errors.

For example, the consequences of programs to increase productivity, such as merit pay, controlled salary levels, and increased class size, are seldom objectively analyzed. As a result, there can be no agreement about whether or not they work. They may be accepted by some campus participants because they appear plausible and consistent with preconceived ideas. If a program is implemented, those who support it may justify that support by selectively—but unconsciously—attaching it to positive changes on campus to which it could arguably be related. The ease with which such inferences can be made can lead people to incorrectly learn that their ideas for improved productivity have been effective. The tendency to see what is expected means that an advocate of a particular program will find it difficult to change his or her opinion and may overlook even strong disconfirming evidence.

Similar factors may affect the degree to which what is learned at one institution may be usefully applied at another. For instance, what is learned about productivity at a research university with a high per-student income may not be applicable at a community college with a small and relatively inflexible budget. In addition, even though programs that are believed to have led to improvements in productivity at one institution can be identified, it is difficult to develop those same programs in other settings.

One popular way to respond to the constraint of learning was to propose that more data be collected and analyzed. While the quest for data seems reasonable, on-campus experiences indicated that such data may not shed light on major productivity issues and may not be used by anyone even if time and energy were devoted to collecting it.

Attention. There were many more problems on every campus than there was time to consider them, so that all respondents had to decide what they would pay attention to. Given the competing demands, attention was not given to many of the issues people believed could increase productivity. At one campus, a review of the entire curriculum was seen as a major need—but it had not been accomplished because of heavy faculty work loads and other pressing issues. As one faculty member lamented, "We could be even more efficient if we reviewed the entire curriculum. Are we offering the right majors? Do our facilities support them? We haven't looked at this for a long time. The reason we haven't done this is time. The faculty is over-loaded."

On some of the campuses where a new president had recently taken office, concern for fund-raising, building administrative teams, or trying to establish new levels of trust and confidence on campus were given priority attention. On others, both routine (i.e., accreditation visits) and nonroutine (i.e., administrative searches) activities acted like sponges and soaked up whatever discretionary time and energy trustees or administrators would otherwise have had. Trustees and administrators (and often faculty as well) knew things they might do to increase productivity but had little time for such endeavors.

Ambiguity. Institutional goals and outcomes were usually so ambiguous that many legitimate interpretations could be made of them. For instance, in the absence of universally accepted indicators, those outside an institution could always see room for improvement, while those inside could find ample evidence that it was already unusually productive. Two processes helped institutions make sense of the ambiguities—the selection of criteria and the determination of peer groups—but those processes presented problems.

Because there were no universally accepted indicators, institutions could select the criteria against which they wished to measure their own productivity. For example, one institution assessed itself as productive because its students did well on standardized exams, were admitted to prestigious graduate and professional schools, and obtained good jobs. The institution could reach its judgment without considering how these achievements could have been related to the entering characteristics of its students or comparing its outcomes to those of similar institutions. Another institution, on the other hand, focused attention on the value-added aspects of its program and discounted academic achievement or test scores. The criterion used was reflected in statements such as, "When you look at what we start out with, and some of the cases you end up with . . . I think we're doing a good job."

In the absence of objective indicators of productivity, institutions believed that the only sensible criterion was comparison with peer institutions. One administrator said, "Efficiency is a relative measure. If your cost is similar to other places of similar or higher status, then you're being efficient." Although the development of peer groups may appear to bring objectivity to assessment of productivity, in fact, peer groups could be defined in many ways. Institutions tended to select peer-group definitions that either supported the belief that they were underfunded or that allowed them to justify their ample funding in terms of the high-quality services they provided.

Satisfaction. On all campuses, productivity was assessed heuristically and intuitively, and to the extent data were available, they were often used to reinforce biases. But despite—or perhaps because of—the lack of objective evidence, most respondents believed themselves to be productive and were generally satisfied with their institution's productivity and therefore had no incentive to change. They believed their institution to be efficient, given the conditions under which it had to operate, and effective, when compared to similar institutions. These beliefs were possible because of the many plausible definitions of input and output and individual self-perceptions about working hard and being effective. Respondents at every campus were able to point with pride to specific instances that justified their sense that the campus was already quite productive or that there had been recent improvements in quality across the board.

Although everyone knew individuals who were unproductive, in general on-campus people saw everyone working as hard as they could. This was probably partially related to a cognitive bias in which immediately available evidence (based on self-assessment or observing others) was given too much credence. Information about comprehensive institutional work-load trends, while less available, would have been more substantiating.

From outside an institution, productivity may have appeared to have remained stable or diminished when measured by common indicators such as cost per unit. But respondents inside saw themselves as more productive despite such data, because they knew that they were working harder than ever. Both perceptions could be accurate. People could be working harder without increasing their output if, for example, the environment changed so that the measured academic achievements of entering students decreased or additional time and effort were required to respond to external demands for accountability. Thus it was possible for institutions to judge themselves more productive while external groups judged them as less so—depending on which data the groups had access to and the definitions they used.

IMPROVING PRODUCTIVITY

As you have just read, productivity in higher education is influenced by an interacting web of administrative policies, environmental pressures, and political processes. The balance among these elements is determined by an institution's history and culture as well as by the cognitive operations that influence judgments made under ambiguous circumstances. Simple interpretations of productivity, which through ignorance or wishful thinking disregard this complex reality, tend to recommend simplistic structures or processes for improvement that are doomed to fail. Productivity in higher education is more a social issue than a technical one and more a political issue than an empirical one.

At least part of the problem is that the debate has not sufficiently disaggregated institutions based on the immense variance in their unit costs. We have not discriminated between increases of financial inputs to institutions that are already among the most wealthy and those that are less affluent. An argument can be made that for poorer institutions increased support is necessary if they are to reach or maintain acceptable levels of quality. Still we continue to search for the philosophers' stone of academic productivity even though it can be argued that we have known for some time what would make institutions more productive. There is an extensive tradition in higher education of proposals to improve productivity that would require no greater technical sophistication than a yellow pad and the ability to count, add, and divide. Thirty years ago, for example, in *Memo to a College Trustee,* Ruml and Morrison calculated the savings that could be generated by thoughtful attention to class-size distributions. Similarly, in *Memo to a College Faculty Member,* McGrath demonstrated the significant cost reductions that could be achieved through relatively minor curriculum changes, and in *Efficiency in Liberal Education,* Bowen and Douglass analyzed the costs of alternative approaches to instructional design. Although there are no contemporary comparative data, it is safe to assume that the productivity improvements recommended by these authors have probably not been achieved—even though the institutions about which they wrote were smaller, simpler, more autonomous, and (probably) more controllable than the average institution today. Knowing some of the things that could be done to increase productivity is one thing; knowing how to implement them is something else.

Simple solutions for improving productivity rely on formulas, draconian brute-force pressures, and threats of external intervention. They may win short-term battles but will almost certainly lose long-term wars. They diminish the commitment of faculty and others who provide the productive services of the institution, maximize short-run effectiveness at the expense of investment in future products, and, according to Trow in *The Public and Private Lives of Public Education,* eliminate the organizational flexibility and general messiness that are essential features of our greatest universities.

More complex solutions take into consideration the multiple and subjective realities of participants on the campuses. These complexities may frustrate the policymaker because they present no easy answers for those who wish to alter campus efficiency and effectiveness, but they also instruct by suggesting what *not* to do.

Based on the evidence collected for this chapter, several generalizations regarding improving productivity in higher education can be made.

1. *Institutions will not attend to matters of productivity that are defined in terms of controlling costs except under the most unusual conditions.*

The costs of higher education are driven by available revenues rather than by concern for efficiency or by the pressures of competition. In fact, for the most part, there is no incentive for institutions to cut costs. In view of faculty salary demands, the need for new and more expensive equipment to support new programs, and the inexorable drive toward qualitative improvements, it would be politically unwise—perhaps even institutionally derelict—for a college president to seek less income than could be obtained. As an administrator explained, increasing income is what enables institutions to be successful: "If there's enough money, or we can get it through fees or endowment, we will continue. The attitude is 'let's not give up anything we have, because it makes us able to do our mission and get high ratings from outsiders.'" Bowen, in *The Costs of Higher Education,* was probably right to suggest that the only way to control costs is to control income.

2. *Productivity structures and processes must be developed and implemented internally.*

Although pressure for cost containment may come from outside sources, effective productivity measures must be developed and implemented internally. This means that there must be significant involvement by both the faculty and the administration.

There were several programs within the institutions studied for this chapter that were believed by campus respondents to have improved productivity—it is important to note, however, that increased productivity was not an expressed purpose of those programs. Although some of the programs were initiated by administrators, all had faculty involvement throughout early planning stages and implementation.

Some of the programs were implemented institution-wide. Faculty leaders endorsed them and often believed that they had been created by the faculty itself or by the administration in response to the faculty's will. These were governed by joint faculty-administration committees, and faculty exhibited a proprietary interest in them.

Other successful productivity programs were department specific. They were almost always initiated by a faculty champion and benefited from the administration's tacit support or benign indifference. At an institution identified by many faculty members as having an autocratic administration, the development of an effective program to reduce attrition was credited to a faculty sponsor. Getting the students and faculty involved—participative management—was believed to have been the only way that productivity could have been increased. The message from these campuses was that unless productivity was the business of the entire campus, productivity improvement efforts would quickly become an exercise in manipulation, subterfuge, and resistance that could absorb time and attention but would have few positive consequences. But making productivity everyone's business would not result from a legislative mandate, a board edict, or a presidential order. Productivity became a concern campuswide when people developed a sense of institutional loyalty, a feeling of shared responsibility, and a commitment to common academic values.

3. *Programs must complement faculty attitudes and values—not conflict with them—if they are to be successful.*

Most of what is produced in higher education is a result of faculty activity. Attempts to increase productivity that are seen as inconsistent with faculty interests will likely lead to reduced effort and lower morale instead of improvements.

Cost-controlling strategies such as larger classes, more part-time faculty, or increased work loads were seen by faculty as having been mindlessly imposed by persons or agencies that had no understanding of the academic enterprise. These kinds of strategies were believed to have a negative effect on productivity because they reduced faculty morale and, consequently, the energy faculty members were willing to commit. In contrast, faculty morale and energy levels increased when faculty members were proud of their institution, believed that their efforts were appreciated and rewarded, felt that they had a stake in institutional decision-making, and were given license and encouragement to experiment with new ideas.

Programs that appeared to be the most effective emphasized superordinate goals consistent with faculty values. For example, the preferred alternative to reducing costs seemed to be improving quality. Quality was a core academic value and faculty did not have to be convinced of its importance. Programs that emphasized commitment to students, concern for learning, and improved scholarship tapped the inherent interests of faculty.

Two institutions studied for this chapter had developed programs that had these characteristics. These institutions had completely different missions, resources, constituencies, presidential tenures, and auspices. Although each program had different objectives, both were strongly supported by experienced and able presidents. Each president had a clear sense of the institution's culture and was seen by faculty as its exemplar. In the developmental phase, presidents gave primary attention to institutionalizing the processes by which faculty and other constituencies would participate. The governance mechanisms that were established gave legislative authority to joint administration-faculty groups, involved faculty members in critical evaluations of their own work and the work of their colleagues, and used outside consultants and experts as part of the process.

Both programs were designed to account for the decentralized nature of academic life and the fact that faculty were more likely to be concerned about departmental issues than institutional matters. Therefore, while both were institution-wide, they emphasized changes in the small subunits that faculty members identified with and could make personal commitments to. On both campuses, administrators were strong public advocates of their institution's progress, faculty members had great pride in their institution's accomplishments, and presidential pronouncements kept the programs visible to the entire campus community.

Finally, and perhaps most important, while administrators in both programs monitored costs through existing budget processes, all programmatic judgments were made on the basis of their contribution to academic quality and student performance. Neither program was designed, nor operated, to reduce expenses. At both institutions testimony from all constituents was unanimous in asserting that the programs had significantly increased and focused the activity level of both faculty and administration.

4. *Productivity is more a state of mind than a structure or a process.*

When interviewed for this chapter a trustee said, "Efficiency is a conscious decision having been made—not rudderless or inertia." An administrator referred to the importance of doing things that make people "think about what it is they are doing and why. That's less likely to happen if it is externally imposed. It's not a mechanical process." Another administrator said, "Every department and every school ought to have a program—a series of activities that they expect will produce a desired, predetermined product. . . . Productivity means how well you produce that student and speaks to the holistic development of the student. If you ask these questions, it works the hell out of people and keeps them busy and excited." All three statements suggest that productivity requires thoughtful reflection on institutional operations and not rote or thoughtless attention.

Perhaps the formula for increased productivity is part "attention" and part just "being there." One administrator who objected to the use of outcome measures believed that productivity could be increased if people spent more time on campus. "If I were a college president," the administrator stated, "one thing I'd be happy to see is people around, in libraries, labs, on weekends." Simply put, productivity may be improved by making the campus a place people want to be.

5. *Sometimes incremental changes may be more successful than comprehensive programs for change.*

Any reasonably perceptive observer can walk onto a college campus and in a day's time uncover myriad unproductive practices—many of which are known to the institution's leaders and staff. Certainly, a competent systems analyst could design structures and processes that would appear to correct these things, but few such proposals result in all the intended positive consequences—more often they bring about unintended, negative results. It happens that sometimes, despite best efforts, little can be done to measurably improve the productivity of an institution. This can be interpreted as a message of despair or as a suggestion that, even when major change is not possible, small improvements can be made.

At each of the institutions that were included in the research for this chapter, leaders were concerned about improving campus programs and were sensitive to issues of cost and performance. Each campus, without exception, had been engaged in base-reallocation activities. Each institution could justifiably point to improvements in quality and efficiency in one or more programs or processes, and in at least two cases these changes were conspicuous. But on most campuses, improvements were limited, focused on organizational subunits, and likely to have had little measurable impact on institutional productivity as a whole. These incremental improvements probably typify the way most organizations change most of the time.

Some of the "smaller" approaches to helping an institution overcome constraints on improved productivity include supporting investment in equipment and personnel to give faculty more time to work with students; providing resources to develop data systems; allowing public-sector institutions more flexibility in how they spend resources; providing support for faculty and administrative in-service development programs; focusing attention on improving quality rather than reducing costs; minimizing the occurrence of budget adjustments, particularly in midyear; supporting and encouraging the development of internal communication systems; creating a climate tolerant of creative failures; supporting institutional leaders rather than working as watchdogs or critics; encouraging reflective self-criticisms; and providing incentives by sharing savings with the units that generate them.

SUMMARY

Colleges and universities are messy institutions in a messy world, but they are also among the most successful organizations in our society. As with all organizations, there exist opportunities for increased efficiency and effectiveness—and institutions of higher education will benefit from responding to them with disciplined intelligence. Nevertheless, considering the rational, cultural, political, and cognitive constraints that currently define its reality, higher education is doing well.

I don't believe that improving productivity in higher education is a problem that requires heroic measures. We should place more reliance on the proven resilience of our colleges and universities and on the best efforts and judgments of their leaders as they respond to the pressures of the marketplace. The perceived lack of productivity in higher education may lie less with our institutions and more with our measurements: money may not be the best measure of the value of services.

Bibliography

Bensimon, E. M. "Viewing the Presidency: Perceptual Congruence Between Presidents and Leaders on Their Campuses." National Center for Postsecondary Governance and Finance, College Park, Maryland, 1988.

Bensimon, E. M., A. Neumann, and R. Birnbaum. *Making Sense of Administrative Leadership: The "L" Word in Higher Education.* Washington: ERIC Clearinghouse on Higher Education, 1989.

Birnbaum, R. *How Colleges Work: The Cybernetics of Academic Organization and Leadership.* San Francisco: Jossey-Bass, 1988.

Bolman, L. G., and T. E. Deal. *Modern Approaches to Understanding and Managing Organizations.* San Francisco: Jossey-Bass, 1984.

Bowen, H. R. *The Costs of Higher Education.* San Francisco: Jossey-Bass, 1980.

Bowen, H. R., and G. K. Douglass. *Efficiency in Liberal Education.* New York: McGraw-Hill, 1971.

Cameron, K. S. "Measuring Organizational Effectiveness in Institutions of Higher Education." *Administrative Science Quarterly,* 23 (1978): 604–32.

——————. "Institutional Effectiveness in Higher Education: An Introduction." *Review of Higher Education,* 9 (1985): 1–4.

Mahoney, T. A. "Productivity Defined: The Relativity of Efficiency, Effectiveness, and Change." *Productivity in Organizations: New Perspectives from Industrial and Organizational Psychology.* J. P. Campbell, Richard J. Campbell, and associates, eds. San Francisco: Jossey-Bass, 1988.

Masland, A. T. "Organizational Culture in the Study of Higher Education." *Review of Higher Education,* 8 (1985): 157–68.

McGrath, E. J. *Memo to a College Faculty Member.* New York: Teachers College, Columbia University, 1961.

Morgan, G. *Images of Organizations.* Beverly Hills: Sage, 1986.

O'Neill, J. *Resource Use in Higher Education: Trends in Inputs and Outputs, 1930–1967.* Berkeley: Carnegie Foundation for the Advancement of Teaching, 1971.

Ruml, B., and D. H. Morrison. *Memo to a College Trustee.* New York: McGraw-Hill, 1959.

Toombs, W. *Productivity: Burden of Success.* Washington: American Association for Higher Education, ERIC/Higher Education Research Report No. 2, 1973.

Trow, M. "The Public and Private Lives of Higher Education." *Daedalus,* 104 (1975): 113–27.

Chapter 3

Improvement Strategies for Administration and Support Services

William F. Massy

Director, Stanford Institute
for Higher Education Research
Stanford University

In a report on the problem of increased research overhead published in the late 1980s, the Association of American Universities brought attention to the need to hold the line on administrative and support costs. Picking up where the AAU left off, William Massy acknowledges the necessity for administrators to improve their own area before they can address the question of productivity in academic departments. In this chapter, Dr. Massy responds to the problem by discussing factors that reduce productivity in administrative and support areas, presenting a step-by-step process for diagnosing such problems and laying out the elements of an effective productivity improvement strategy.

We are all familiar with the history of cost escalation in colleges and universities and the negative impression this has made on the general public. For example, an article entitled "The Untouchables" in the November 30, 1987, issue of *Forbes* asked the question: "Are colleges picking our pockets?" According to this piece, "Efficiency and cost cutting are demanded of unions and industry. Even government is under pressure to deliver value for the dollar. Why then does higher education get away with delivering a deteriorating product at ever increasing prices?" As Chester E. Finn Jr. has

This work was sponsored by the National Center for Postsecondary Governance and Finance at the University of Maryland College Park.

stated in "Judgment Time for Higher Education: In the Court of Public Opinion," the court of public opinion is concluding that institutions of higher education are not as efficient or productive as they should be.

Parents are becoming more and more concerned about whether they will be able to afford college, and, indeed, many are asking themselves whether the financial sacrifice associated with sending a child to a high-priced private college is warranted. Cost increases at public institutions often trigger sharp political debates, and students everywhere demonstrate against tuition hikes at their schools. Higher education officials argue that the money is needed to maintain or increase quality, but they are challenged by those who demand to know if the quality gained is worth the price.

There are two general explanations of why education costs keep rising. They are higher education's "cost disease" and its "growth force."

Cost disease accounts for expenses escalating faster than the rate of inflation. Most operating costs in education are wage driven, and competition in the labor market links a school's salary increases to the rate of productivity improvement in the national economy. The theory is borne out by the behavior of the higher education price index (HEPI) in relation to the consumer price index (CPI). The former rose at an annual rate of 6.4 percent for the period 1961–86, while in the same period the latter rose by 5.3 percent—a difference of 1.1 percent. (The differential was 1.0 percent for the decade of the 1960s; 1.0 percent for the 1970s when, in an effort to cope with the oil crisis, higher education allowed salaries to lag; and 2.3 percent for the 1980s, when salaries caught up.) The cost-disease explanation points out that as long as a school's student-faculty ratio remains constant, its unit costs will tend to grow in real terms. Steady erosion of student-faculty ratios will have adverse effects on quality.

Growth force applies to the phenomenon of budgets growing faster than can be accounted for by mere cost increases. It is usually due to the addition of new academic programs and the reluctance of administrators to dismantle old programs and reallocate funds to the new ones. The need for new academic programs springs from the dynamism of knowledge development and the creativity of college and university faculty and students. An institution that fails to innovate will soon fall behind—an outcome that university officers rightly seek to avoid. Add-ons are also the rule in administration and support services. The cost of meeting a new government regulation, for instance, or supplying a newly demanded service is usually layered on top of existing costs.

More specific reasons why college and university costs are continually increasing include the constant need for new technology, rising utility costs, and, of course, the accretion of organizational slack. Whatever the causes, current fund expenditures per full-time equivalent (FTE) student in all higher education institutions grew at an annual rate of 1.4 percent over the HEPI between 1975–76 and 1985–86. (The figures for public and private institution were 1.2 percent and 1.6 percent, respectively.) Much ingenuity, energy, management skill, and motivation are needed to innovate and meet new requirements with constant or declining resources, and it appears to critics of higher education that these have not been forthcoming.

Why, they ask, are new programs, functions, and services usually add-ons to budgets instead of replacements for existing activities? Why don't investments in new facilities and equipment reduce costs rather than add to them? Why don't institutional leaders put more emphasis on productivity? Why is there so much pressure to increase quality and so little to improve cost effectiveness? Why do support-service departments seem to suffer the same productivity malaise as the academic departments with seemingly less justification?

I have chosen to focus on this last question and offer some suggestions for improving administrative and support service productivity.

GROWTH OF ADMINISTRATION AND SUPPORT COSTS

Administration and support costs amount to some 30 percent of education and general (E&G) expenditures at public institutions and over 40 percent at private institutions, according to Arthur M. Hauptman's report, "Why Are College Charges Increasing? Looking into the Various Explanations." As shown in Table 1, most indirect costs (other than for libraries) are growing faster than direct costs. Administration and student services are the growth-rate leaders in both public and private institutions, and their effect on budgets is compounded by the fact that between them they account for 25 percent of E&G expenses. Most institutions would do well to focus on these service areas when looking at costs. Although all the categories in the table are important to consider, demonstrable progress in containing administration and support costs is a necessary precursor to addressing the question of productivity in academic departments.

Growth-Rate Analysis

The first step in getting a grip on administrative and support costs is to systematically observe the pattern of cost increases during the preceding

TABLE 1
Growth Rates of Key Expense Categories for Public and Private Higher
Education 1975/1976 to 1985/1986.

	Public	Private
Indirect		
Administration	5.0%	7.6%
Student Services	4.9%	8.3%
Libraries	0.4%	1.6%
Operations and maintenance	3.4%	5.0%
Direct		
Instruction	2.7%	4.5%
Research	5.1%	3.5%
Public service	3.6%	7.0%

Computed from "Why Are College Charges Increasing? Looking into the Various Explanations,"
Table 4, by Arthur M. Hauptman.

three to five years. (A variation on this procedure is to calculate increases in
FTE employees by organizational unit, based on payroll records for a fixed
date in each benchmark year.) The analysis can proceed as follows: (1) from
the pattern of cost increases, develop a chart outlining the administration
and support services organization; (2) extract data for two or more benchmark years according to this chart; (3) calculate the annualized growth for
each organizational unit in the tree; and (4) focus attention on the high-
growth units. If no assignable cause for high growth can be found, the unit is
a prime candidate for cost reduction. It is hard to determine in advance what
organizational level to look at, so it is best to start at a fairly minor level in
the organization and then look at more levels until you can reach conclusions about what is meaningful growth.

The Cambridge, Massachusetts-based MAC Group of management consultants performed such an analysis for a midwestern research university a
few years ago. The operating units were ranked according to growth rate in
expenditures, and attention was focused on those that fell outside the norm
for the organization—the outliers. Special study was made of the outliers
that showed higher-than-average expenses. On closer investigation, it
turned out that some of the extremes were due to readily assignable causes
such as reorganization or a high-level management decision to add to service levels. In other cases, the growth seemed to be due to steady accretion.

Marginal Cost

Sometimes indirect costs are driven by changes in the scale of direct activities like instruction and research. The slope of this relation is, of course, the marginal or incremental cost of the indirect activity with respect to the direct one. Everyone who has taken an economics course knows about marginal costs, but there seem to be few applications for the concept in colleges and universities. There are, however, three ways in which one can examine higher education's marginal costs: the regression method, the fixed- and variable-cost method, and the incremental-cost method. Briefly, the first is a statistical procedure usually based on time-series data. The second assigns each element of expense into a fixed or variable (i.e., marginal) component based on a detailed understanding of the process involved. The third attempts to identify and quantify the components of cost that vary with a given external variable.

Information about marginal costs helps interpret the growth-rate analysis results described earlier. It may be possible, for instance, to normalize some of the growth rates for changes in the cost-driving activities. As an example, when looking at growth rates in an accounting office, one might observe that transactions (T) are growing at x percent per year, that costs (C) are growing at y percent over the university's index of cost rise for continuing activities, and that marginal costs (MC) are about z percent of total cost. The following formula can be used to calculate the change in cost expected in that accounting office on the basis of the changed transaction volume.

$$\Delta T = xT$$
$$\Delta C = yC$$
$$MC = z\ C/T$$
$$\Rightarrow \text{normalized } y = (1+y)/(1+xz)$$

Suppose $x = 3$ percent, $y = 1.5$ percent, and $z = 30$ percent. Substituting these numbers in the above formula yields normalized $y = 1.015/(1 + 0.03 \times 0.30)$ = 1.006, a growth rate of only 0.6 percent. The difference between 1.5 percent net expansion and 0.6 percent net expansion adjusted for volume growth would make a big difference in one's thinking about what has been happening in that office.

This example assumes that there is only one cost-driving variable. Of course there may be multiple variables, in which case, to separate their individual effects the regression method may be required. It is best, however, to begin with a single cost-driver variable for each organizational unit. (It may be necessary to disaggregate another level or two to find a unit with one main driver.) There is, of course, no harm in having different cost drivers for different organizational units—it is required if the analysis is to be comprehensive. The preliminary specifications for an institution-wide cost study at Stanford, for instance, include the following cost drivers.

- Employee head count—used in the controller's office for payroll and in personnel services.
- Accounting transactions—used in the controller's office for general accounting.
- Number of separate funds—used for fund accounting and in the treasurer's office.
- Building square footage—used in operations and maintenance, security, and health and safety.

Remember, these are not the only cost drivers. The important thing is to start somewhere and build an internally consistent set of measures that can normalize observed and requested expense growth rates. The model can be refined according to individual needs, but even rough marginal cost measures are useful.

How can conclusions be reached about growth-rate outliers that cannot be explained by cost drivers? First, identify some other assignable cause that is acceptable from the standpoint of productivity—for example, new regulations. It is important not to accept rationalizations. Much of what is explained away as increased complexity turns out to be bureaucratic accretion, the nemesis of productivity. The rule should be to take a hard look at all the outliers and some units that are not outliers but, because of known external forces that might have been expected to reduce their work load, should have been. The second step is to examine the units for productivity-degrading factors.

FACTORS THAT DEGRADE PRODUCTIVITY

Left to themselves, most organizations are not only sluggish in adopting productivity-enhancing innovations but actually tend to self-destruct in regard to productivity. This self-destruction can be compared to the thermodynamic concept of entropy. In the state of lowest potential, any closed system will "run down" in the sense that its energy will eventually distribute itself evenly. The only way to counter this tendency is to introduce new energy from the outside to keep the system efficient. Before discussing ways that leaders in higher education can introduce energy and information to their organizations and avoid running down productivity, however, I'd like to first examine the three main destructive forces.

Organizational Slack

Organizational slack can stem from simple inattention to efficiency—in which case "fat" is an apt descriptor. Slack can also arise when employees are prevented from performing effectively or when their personal goals are inappropriately substituted for those of the organization. The latter situation, known as resource diversion, gives rise to the view that people will pursue their own interests at the expense of the organization's at every opportunity. Substitution of personal for organizational goals can take the form of loafing, appropriating the organization's resources for personal use, or, perhaps, becoming obsessed with one's own rights and privileges.

Slack is not always bad. Too strong an emphasis on efficiency can demotivate employees and possibly stunt innovation. The beneficial aspects of slack are even more important in higher education than in industry, and they are most important in research universities where innovation must be a way of life. This is why faculty sometimes question the overzealous pursuit of efficiency in academic departments. (Their concerns are reinforced by the fact that what may seem like slack to an outsider is actually the contemplation necessary to produce new discoveries.)

On the administrative and support side of colleges and universities though, the value of slack is about the same as it is for business and government—some slack is a good investment for the future but too much is an unacceptable drag on current operations. James March, in his article "Emerging Developments in the Study of Organizations," put it well when he wrote:

> Under good conditions, slack search generates ideas, many of them too risky for immediate adoption. When conditions change, such ideas are available as potential solutions to new problems. An organization is able to meet brief periods of decline by drawing on discoveries generated, but overlooked, during better times. A prolonged period of adversity or of exceptional efficiency in avoiding slack depletes the reservoir and leaves the organization vulnerable.

Slack tends to build up in good times and be squeezed out when times turn bad. J. Paul Austin, chairman of the United States Steel Corporation during the 1950s, once told me that U.S. Steel was "like a big bear—building up fat during economic booms and then hibernating, maintaining itself by shedding fat, during recessions." The cyclical process seems inevitable, but if it is not controlled, the slack may build to dysfunctional levels during good times and the eventual squeezing out may be incomplete. An organization should restructure itself to improve during the course of each cycle rather than simply allow history to repeat itself over and over again.

Accretion of Unnecessary Tasks

Everyone can be busy performing his or her assigned duties with energy and intelligence, and yet the organization as a whole may lack productivity. The key is in deciding what tasks are to be performed or, more precisely, in determining whether the tasks, taken separately and as an ensemble, contribute optimally to the long-range purpose of the whole organization.

Productivity is a measure of effectiveness. It reflects an assessment of the usefulness of what is being done, as well as the ratio of outputs to inputs, per se. Effectiveness, however, is not the same as efficiency, which is based on the narrower measure of the resources required to accomplish a particular task without regard to the task's ultimate value.

There are many reasons for the accretion of tasks. Workers or managers may lack competence and thus create unnecessary work for others—when a personnel department must clean up an employee relations mess left by an overbearing supervisor, for instance. A work unit might create unnecessary tasks by suboptimizing their resources, which can result in a redundancy of effort—as when two departments teach the same subject, each to half the optimal number of students. If not corrected decisively, certain types of incompetence and suboptimization can become the organizational norm.

Escalating spirals of administrative interactions are another prime cause of task accretion. A good person is hired to perform a certain task. That task results in the discovery of new problems, creating the need to perform additional tasks. Others in the organization are drawn in since they must respond to the new initiatives. Coordinating everyone's efforts means that time is being spent in meetings. Soon, additional people must be hired to keep up with the increased work load. They, in turn, find new problems and create work for others—thus perpetuating the spiral. As Jane Hannaway phrased it in her study *Supply Creates Demands: An Organizational Process View of Administrative Expansion,* "The supply of administrators creates its own demand." This problem can be seen not only in education but in all sectors of business and government. For example, government bureaucracies grow inevitably and inexorably as they respond to new sets of problems. These problems beget new organizations or increase the number of layers in existing organizations. This is one reason why heavily regulated industries have many layers of management.

Instituting procedures to correct problems without periodically examining how the procedures can be refined is a common cause of task accretion. Another cause can be two procedures developed for different purposes that cover much of the same ground. Whatever the situation, it is certain that continual layering of new procedures to address new problems will in time degrade productivity. Conscious decisions and much energy are required to reverse the trend and strip away the layers or their cumulative effect will stifle organizational effectiveness at an ever-increasing rate.

Function Lust

Controllers think that their job is important and tend to want to do more of it. The same is true for auditors, planners, builders, landscape architects, lawyers, and even minute-takers in the myriad meetings that characterize colleges and universities. Student-service professionals, librarians, and computer experts are not exempt either. All can make a perfectly plausible case for how the institution could benefit by more being produced from their specialty. While the phrase "function lust" is perjorative, the motives of those who perpetuate the notion are, at least in their own eyes, pure. All these functions are important; otherwise the institution would not have created job openings for them in the first place. The problem is that specialists are not necessarily in the best position to gauge their own importance in relation to other institutional needs. They can do a good job of assessing absolute importance but are less successful in determining relative priorities and in negotiating trade-offs with other functions.

An outgrowth of function lust is the incentive to increase one's job responsibilities and get promoted, which also contributes to administrative task accretion. Job classification systems that offer advancement on the basis of budget size or the number of people supervised are particularly prone to this malady. Organizations whose managers permit "turf wars" invite accretion because the incentives are to staff up in order to beat competing departments instead of trying to cooperate with them. A certain amount of competition can be healthy, but too much is wasteful.

DIAGNOSING PROBLEMS

While information about expenditure or staff growth rates for organizational units can point toward areas where productivity is suspect, these quantitative measures cannot provide information on *why*. Informal managerial evaluation is the method of choice for diagnosing problems. There is no substitute for "management by walking around," especially in areas where there is reason to suspect subtly hidden difficulties. Unfortunately, though, even the most perceptive managers may well miss systemic issues—i.e., those that involve more than one function or unit—if they rely solely on intuitive processes. More formal approaches can be of greater effectiveness, especially if the organization is embarking on a major productivity enhancement effort.

The Process-by-Function Matrix

Certain key administration and support operations are common to all colleges or universities of a given size and type, regardless of how they are organized. These operations can be displayed in a process-by-function matrix where function refers to activities generally associated with an organizational unit. A hypothetical example of such a matrix is presented in Table 2.

The important processes of hiring and paying people are depicted in the first two columns of the matrix. Each process is initiated by an operating department. (The initiating department may be either academic or nonacademic.) The action must then be approved by the appropriate dean or, in the case of nonacademic units, the vice president or his or her delegate. Actions on high-level positions must be approved by the president or by the provost's office. In many cases, the Affirmative Action officer must approve the new hire as well. The personnel department will review and render an opinion sometime during the process. Though personnel may not have the last word, its view is taken into account by the aforementioned decision makers. The payment screening section of the controller's office may be asked to verify that funds are available and that the hiring or salary is consistent with the project budget and with other contractual requirements if this is a sponsored agreement. Of course, the payroll department and the general accounting department get involved in processing the transaction when it finally comes to pass.

Often the process will loop back to involve a given function more than once. Consider the process of purchasing, for example. This is done many thousands of times annually and, while it would seem to be a simple task, it actually is very complicated. The transaction usually originates in an academic or operating department. The typical pattern is for a purchase order to

TABLE 2
A Hypothetical Process-by-Function Matrix.

Function	Human Resources		Purchasing (general)	Purchasing (equipment)		Submitting Research Proposals	Procurement Contracts	
	Hiring People	Paying People		Gov't. Projects	Univ. Funds		Gov't. Projects	Univ. Funds
Academic or operating department	✓	✓	✓	✓	✓	✓	✓	✓
School dean or vice president	✓	✓	✓	✓	✓	✓	✓	✓
President or provost	✓	✓			✓			✓
Dean of research				✓		✓	✓	
Affirmative Action office	✓	✓						
Personnel office								
Employment	✓							
Compensation		✓						
Employee relations		✓						
Controller's office								
Payment screening	✓		✓	✓	✓		✓	✓
Accounts payable			✓	✓	✓		✓	✓
Payroll	✓	✓						
General accounting	✓	✓	✓	✓	✓		✓	✓
Sponsored projects office						✓		
Legal office							✓	✓
Facilities office							✓	✓
Procurement department			✓	✓	✓			

Computed from "Why Are College Charges Increasing? Looking into the Various Explanations," by Arthur M. Hauptman.

be checked for fund availability by the payment screening group and then be sent to procurement for vendor selection and, if applicable, negotiation of price and terms. Procurement writes a purchase order and notifies the vendor, the originating department, and accounts payable. The order is shipped directly to the originating department, which is responsible for matching the purchase order to the packing slip and notifying procurement and accounts payable that the desired goods have been received and are satisfactory. In the meantime, the vendor sends a bill to accounts payable, which matches it to the appropriate receiving notice. The bill is paid (perhaps after a lag to optimize the financial float) and the transaction is entered into the general ledger. It then appears on the originating department's budget and expenditure statement. Is it any wonder that faculty complain about slow turnaround and departmental administrators are driven to their wits' end trying to keep track of outstanding expenditure commitments?

Similar descriptions could be given for the other processes in the matrix. Though this is only a hypothetical example, most people who know colleges and universities will recognize it as a familiar pattern.

Process Flowcharts

The next step is to develop flowcharts for the processes shown in the matrix. Flowcharts help to organize information about the order in which activities are typically or necessarily performed. Useful insights can be added by showing the range of delay times and perhaps the number of man-hours required to transact each step. The approach should be pragmatic; use a level of detail that illuminates the process, not one that obfuscates it into a maze of unimportant detail. Remember, these are *management displays,* not engineering or computer program specifications. Their purpose is strategic. They are not meant to provide detailed instructions for workers or first-line supervisors. In short, the process flowchart provides essential information about the order in which the gross tasks that make up a process are (or should be) performed, not about how each task should be performed. Each flowchart should take up no more than a single letter-sized page, so that it will fit into a ring binder.

Importance, Reliability, and Redundancy

With the flowchart created, I am ready to turn to diagnosis, which begins with the analysis of importance, reliability, and redundancy. (I have decided to call this IRR, partly because it does provide an "internal rate of return.") The IRR tests are applied to each element of the flowchart.

Because it was included in the process-by-function matrix, the process as a whole has already passed a general test determining its importance. But this is not necessarily the case for its individual elements. The first stage is to scrutinize each step of the process. Tasks that have accreted into the system will not automatically pass if the test is performed rigorously.

One of the main impediments to purging tasks is the argument that deleting a step will degrade the quality of the process. Quality is a loaded word at colleges and universities, and one should not allow that assertion to trump the question of importance—even if the assertion is demonstrably true. The answer lies in recognizing that there are two kinds of quality.

- *Design quality* is the quality designed into the product or service. A BMW has greater design quality than, say, a Ford, and it is more expensive. For some purposes and purses, the BMW represents the best price-quality trade-off; for others, the Ford wins out. It is possible even to construct examples where the Ford is better in absolute terms—regardless of price. Driving in high crime areas or where parts and specially trained mechanics are hard to find are two cases in point. The key idea is that more design quality is *not* always better; it needs to be calibrated to the task or situation at hand.

- *Implementation quality* deals with how well the product or service meets its specifications. If the product is to be a Ford, let it be a well-built Ford. It should be the same whether assembled Monday morning or Wednesday afternoon—no lemons allowed. American industry has learned the hard way that implementation quality should always be maximized. "Do it right the first time" is an important principle both for customer satisfaction and for productivity. Everyone can take pride in producing the best possible implementation quality, but not everyone need aspire to build BMWs.

Taking advantage of higher education's reverence for quality in order to enhance implementation quality is a good thing. Allowing this reverence to mandate unneeded levels of design quality in administration and support services is not. Therefore, one should go through each process flowchart and ask whether the tasks are specified at the minimum acceptable level of design quality. High implementation quality should be insisted on, but academic program needs should rule out unnecessarily expensive work specifications in the administrative and support areas. Implementation quality rarely increases costs significantly. Indeed, an institution probably is paying for this kind of quality anyway, and the only question is whether it is getting its money's worth. Implementation quality is obtained by hiring good people, training them well, and providing good leadership and supervision.

Although reliability is related to design quality and implementation quality, it is worthy of separate consideration for two reasons. First, certain designs will be unreliable even with perfect implementation—these should be avoided if the penalty for failure is even remotely high. Second, issues of reliability tend to be systemic rather than oriented toward the individual process elements.

The assessment of total quality cost (TQC) is being used by many companies as a way to consider the reliability question. The objective is to understand what is being spent on maintaining reliability (that is, preventing failures) and correcting failures. Only by looking carefully at both sides of the equation can a reasonable judgment be made about the optimal reliability. In one case, some 80 percent of cost was due to failure, suggesting that the best trade-off might be to spend more on prevention. The trade-off can go the other way, too. An occasional accounting error that can be corrected later is not as consequential as having a part not work as designed or, worse yet, fail in use. Health and safety, systemic financial control weaknesses, and personnel-policy problems are probably the most worrisome risks— the first for obvious reasons, the second because disallowances and defalcations can be very costly, and the last because of the possibility of class-action lawsuits. The total cost of quality should be assessed for each of the processes included in the matrix.

Redundancy is a clear waste of resources unless it is needed for reliability. Redundancy tends to build up as a by-product of administrative task accretion, and it takes conscious effort and energy to identify and eliminate it. This is basically a common-sense matter: go through the process flowchart and simply ask whether each task is also done somewhere else. If the answer is yes, then question whether the redundancy is needed to contain risk (i.e., for reliability) and how much the risk would be increased if it were eliminated. Often the same risks are mitigated several times in complex systems. One can be more vigorous in rooting out redundancies in processes where the risks of failure are in terms of individual transactions rather than systemic operations.

It is also important to determine whether each process should be centralized or decentralized. Some processes are so critical in terms of the need for precise procedures and quality control that they must be centralized in order to achieve the best performance or to contain risks. Others are better left to the creativity and initiative of those closest to them. More situations probably fall into the latter category than one might think, but each instance requires careful analysis. Generally, one dictum is applicable: decide whether a process must be centralized or whether it can be decentralized and then insist that things be done that way. Do not allow a decentralized process to drift toward centralization because of task accretion by staff groups or second-guessing by upper-level line managers. Such behavior can produce a heavy drag on productivity.

Technology

Once it is clear that only essential tasks are being performed, the next question is whether they can be performed more efficiently. Given a fixed set of tasks, substituting capital for labor is the classic approach for improving productivity, and the second industrial revolution (a phrase coined by Herbert A. Simon in the article "The Steam Engine and the Computer: What Makes Technology Revolutionary") represented by information technology provides unusual opportunities. Volumes have been written about the advantages and pitfalls of office automation, so I will limit myself to only a few points.

- Don't try to automate work processes exactly as they are being done by conventional means. The result will nearly always be a more expensive and less satisfactory product than can be obtained by changing work flows to fit the new opportunities. (This is true especially if packaged software is available to do some or all of the job.)
- Strive to input data once only, as close to their original source as possible. Also, minimize paper flow and the need for multiple files. This not only increases the original cost of the job, but adds additional costs if conflicting information requires reconciliation.
- Don't try to get the process exactly right the first time. Modern software development tools permit systems to evolve as people gain experience with them. Often it is best to build a working prototype that will evolve during the project. This avoids endless arguments about once-and-for-all decisions that are so familiar in traditional development environments.

In the long run, automation can cure the cost disease by substituting a resource whose unit cost is declining in real terms for one whose unit cost is constantly increasing. Sometimes the up-front investment is hard to justify, and it certainly is necessary to be discriminating in terms of proposals. Still, the college or university that is not investing in information technology is likely to be left behind in terms of productivity.

Optimizing Staff Allocations

As with law, accounting, and consulting firms, colleges and universities rely on the services of highly trained professionals—in their support staff as well as their faculty. Productivity improvement in professional-service firms is obtained mainly by substituting less expert and hence less costly people for those with higher levels of expertise. Senior partners leverage their time with that of partners, associates, and research assistants. The cardinal rule is "Always use the least-expert resource that can do the job." Many colleges and universities spend substantial sums on support staff who directly leverage faculty time. Additional sums are spent for lower-level staff who support higher-level people all through administrative and support areas.

Time leveraging in colleges and universities is a double-edged sword. The advantages are the same as in the case of professional firms. However, more leverage is not desirable unless it leads to savings elsewhere. Under what circumstances do such substitutions increase productivity? The answer is easy when talking about for-profit enterprises such as law or consulting firms; the substitution is productive if and only if it increases the partners' income. For colleges and universities the problem is much more difficult because there is no profit measure and, of course, most administrative and support-service outputs are intangible. Individuals often want additional support in order to ease their burdens or to enrich their jobs by unloading repetitive tasks they feel they have fully mastered. The potential for task accretion furthers this phenomenon by offering a ready menu of interesting additional things to do.

THE NEED FOR MANAGEMENT INTERVENTION

Insights into how to diagnose the factors that inhibit productivity in administrative and support services lead to the question "What can be done about them?" What are needed are managerial interventions that afford the possibility of mitigating or reversing the inhibiting factors and that unleash the forces that will enhance productivity and allow more resources to flow to academic operations.

Many of the diagnostic steps discussed in the previous section contain, within themselves, a blueprint for management intervention. The solutions for certain problems are obvious once their existence is understood. Unfortunately, however, a straightforward problem-by-problem attack on productivity often fails to achieve the expected result. The complex interactions among the productivity-inhibiting factors and the people problems associated with change require a carefully thought-out and integrated management intervention strategy.

The growth of medical costs could not be contained until the cost-plus rules of Medicare and Medicaid were amended to establish limits on how much the government would pay for a given procedure or hospital stay. Airline, railroad, and phone companies could not strip away unneeded layers of management and other impediments to productivity until deregulation converted cost-plus into competitive pricing. U.S. industry as a whole could not streamline itself until foreign competition made it a virtual necessity. Similarly, the add-on spiral in higher education must be broken if costs are to be contained. The continued layering of program on program, cost on cost, will sooner or later cause critics of higher education to shift from rhetoric to action. It is better for correction to be accomplished within the academy than imposed from outside. The experience of the medical profession, which a decade ago was seen as singularly unresponsive to the issue of cost containment, supports this thesis.

To arrest the cost-plus spiral higher education must:

- end cost-plus pricing and place strict limits on spending growth, which, in effect, will simulate the discipline of the marketplace; and
- establish planning and resource-allocation processes and incentives to enhance innovation and stimulate resource reallocation from areas with low productivity to those with greater potential.

In other words, the message is "say no, but don't *just* say no." Higher education must simultaneously enforce spending constraints and make sure that its governance and management processes can generate productivity improvement to fund needed innovation.

College and university managers must provide the transitional leadership needed to give productivity high priority—high enough to offset inevitable bureaucratic forces. This requires vision and team building as well as the more traditional applications of legitimate power, tangible incentives, and analytical problem solving. It amounts to answering the question "What must be done in addition to saying no for the institution to change positively?"

The lesson from industry is that while resource constraints are a necessary condition for unleashing productivity improvement and innovation, they are not sufficient. Financial pressure by itself can crush initiative or create conflict over shares of a fixed or shrinking pie. The challenge is to mitigate these effects and turn the financial pressure into a driving force instead of a crushing burden.

TABLE 3
Gaining Productivity.

It is not easy for colleges and universities to increase productivity. The incentives in an academic culture point toward improving quality; there are few obvious incentives for focusing on efficiency and cost effectiveness. It is possible, however, for institutions to contain costs. Under the right conditions, cost containment can trigger increased productivity, thereby helping to achieve improvement in quality.

I believe that there are four conditions necessary for improving productivity.

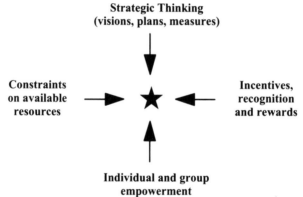

Resource Constraints

Resource constraints can be the driving force behind an institution's decision to increase efficiency and productivity. Most educational leaders press hard to enhance quality, but without the effect of resource constraints there is no incentive to consider cost effectiveness in relation to quality. It is no accident that institutions that regard themselves as relatively well-off financially find it hard to increase productivity, even though they have some of the best human and technological resources for tackling the problem.

Individual and Group Empowerment

Productivity improvement depends on the initiatives and skills of faculty and staff on both the individual and the group levels. They are the ones who are most familiar with the work process and who will implement any day-to-day changes. Faculty and staff must be empowered to lead the institution through its difficult choices. Empowerment means believing that one *can* and *should* make a difference and possessing or having access to the skills and resources needed to do the job.

Incentives, Recognition, and Rewards

Incentives and rewards can be offered in the context of tight resource constraints. In fact, they do not need to be monetary or even tangible. They should, however, be devised to encourage workers to think positively about productivity. It is very important to avoid inadvertently creating incentives that undermine productivity. Personnel reductions that are directly attributable to productivity improvement often decrease the potential for additional gains. Recognizing and celebrating a good result or a good effort is also essential. For example, school administrations should recognize faculty efforts to develop new and more productive teaching methods when setting salaries and making promotion and tenure decisions.

Strategic Thinking

The institution's leaders must engage in strategic thinking about productivity improvement. They must define what they mean by gaining productivity and make clear that it is an important part of their vision for the institution. They must develop plans and programs for embedding the vision in the organizational culture at the working level. They must also provide the concepts and support necessary for empowering people to develop and implement productivity-enhancing initiatives. They must arrange for the right incentives, recognition, and rewards and make sure there is follow-through across the organization.

All four conditions are necessary. Without incentives there will be few faculty and staff initiatives. Without strong conceptual leadership, those initiatives will lack focus, coherence, and staying power. Without faculty and staff initiatives, central visions and plans will stagnate because they lack connection to the actual work process and saliency for the people who would have to implement change. Finally, without a clear and binding resource constraint, the drive for quality and the incentives, recognitions, and rewards associated with quality dominate the objective of gaining productivity.

Adapted from the author's contribution to the article "Double Trouble," which was published in the September 1989 issue of *Policy Perspectives.*

Presentation of a coherent and integrated management intervention strategy is beyond the scope of this chapter, but I will describe some of the elements that have to be included in such a strategy. I hope that this will provide practical advice to higher education executives who are charged with productivity enhancement in the administrative and support service areas.

ELEMENTS OF A PRODUCTIVITY-ENHANCING STRATEGY

Table 3 above provides a paradigm for gaining productivity improvement. It sets forth the interactions among four elements: resource constraints; strategic thinking (visions, plans, measures); incentives, recognition, and rewards; and individual and group empowerment.

Resource Constraints

Approaching the illustration in Table 3 from the nine-o'clock position immediately reveals the problem—in this context, it might better be described as the "opportunity"—of resource constraints. Meeting these constraints must become a major organizational objective, in effect the enactment of environmental limits by the organization.

Strategic Vision

Organizations, especially complex ones, need a common sense of direction, a way for the organization to manage what Stanley M. Davis in *Future Perfect* has called its "beforemath." A good strategic vision can provide this, exerting a pull to the future that permits people to move with sufficient common purpose to accomplish complex goals over a long period of time. Likewise, a shared paradigm about the organization's technological, market, and financial settings and its internal dynamics and management processes allows individuals to work toward a common goal with more independence than would be possible if they operated on different theories.

One of the most important advantages of a shared strategic vision is that

---

TABLE 4
Sample Vision Elements from the Service Industry.

Externally-oriented Elements	Internally-oriented Elements
• How does the service concept propose to meet customer needs?	• What are common characteristics of employee groups?
• What is good service? Does the proposed concept provide it?	• How important are each of these groups to the delivery of service?
• What efforts are required to bring client service expectations and capabilities into alignment?	• What needs does each group have?
• What are the important features of the delivery system?	• How does the service concept propose to meet employee needs?
• How can the actual and perceived differences between the value and cost of services be maximized?	• To what extent are the concept and the delivery system for serving important employee groups internally consistent?
• Where will investments be made and efforts concentrated?	• To what extent have employees been involved in the design of the concept and the delivery system?

Adapted from Exhibits I and II in James L. Heskett's "Lessons from the Private Sector."

---

it makes large-scale organizational change possible over a much longer period of time than would otherwise be possible. Such changes are more likely to require cultural adaptation than simpler changes that deal with individual operations or specific skills and routines. Cultural adaptation requires more time to accomplish. Sometimes the time scale is measured in years, during which memories fade and management turns over. A good strategic vision, well articulated and fully internalized as part of the organization's sense of subjective reality, provides the compass to keep the change process on course.

Strategic vision can be externally oriented or internally oriented, and, according to James L. Heskett's "Lessons from the Private Sector," most organizations need both. The former is usually concerned with what is to be accomplished vis-a-vis the outside environment—i.e., clients, competitors, or suppliers of capital. The latter concerns itself more with how the work will be accomplished and the organization's planning and management processes. Some examples of external and internal vision elements based on the service industry are presented in Table 4. Service-industry experience has much relevance for college and university administration and support services, which are dedicated to serving clients both inside and outside the academy.

Vision is created and promulgated through analysis and communication and by acting out the vision. For mid-level managers and rank-and-file employees, the latter can be furthered through carefully designed training sessions. On the next page, Table 5 presents the results of service training in the Stanford finance division as reported to me by my staff. The benefits of the session included empowerment through confidence building and skill development as well as the creation of a more powerful shared vision of the what, why, and how of providing good service. Extensive feedback from the participants and from their clients confirmed management's assessment that the program was highly successful.

Empowerment

While strategic vision provides a shared sense of what should be done, empowerment provides a powerful force for making things happen—thus providing a new way to think about productivity and change. A recent retreat for my senior finance staff began with a discussion entitled "Empowering Ourselves: What Can I Do to Create a Stanford of the Future to Which I Am Committed?" The investigation began with the meaning of work.

TABLE 5
Results of the Stanford Finance Service Training Sessions.

Good service reinforced as a priority

- Support from top management was made visible in the sessions.
- Importance of good service to clients was recognized.

Clients identified and client relations enhanced through client interviews.

Services clarified and defined

- Unnecessary services were eliminated.
- Valued services were acknowledged.
- Service strengths and issues were identified.

Service skills reviewed

- Characteristics of good and bad service were discussed (accessibility, follow-through, courtesy).
- Effects of Stanford culture on service was examined.

Team building among group members was significantly enhanced (this was the first exposure to team building for some groups).

Self-image of work groups was improved through understanding their contribution to Stanford.

Communications examined

- Work group members in the sessions improved their communications.
- Departmental communications were improved by means of interviews.
- Managers attended sessions and were interviewed.
- Ongoing direct client feedback was initiated.

Many specific service improvements were put in place.

Improvement suggestions identified

- Service improvement plans were developed by every group.
- Management team committed to following up on issues presented by the work groups.

Participants learned that most people work in order to meet some combination of the following objectives.

- To make a living
- To express deepest values
- To create an organization of one's own choosing
- To fulfill potential
- To discover identity

Only the first entry on the list regards work as a means to an end. The others regard it as tapping intrinsic needs. Surprising gains in productivity are possible when these needs are aligned with those of the organization.

The empowered organization contrasts sharply with the traditional, patriarchal organization. Work in the latter tends to be directed toward gaining the approval of one's superiors (the patriarchs), which leads to undue concern about promotion, avoidance of risk, and control of one's work environment. Attention is directed upward (What does the boss think?) and risk is diversified by name-dropping and diffusing responsibility. Management style is often manipulative and calculating. In the empowered organization, however, work means contributing to important shared goals, mastering important skills, finding meaning in thought and action, acting out one's sense of integrity, and having a positive impact on people.

Table 6 depicts what is generally expected from an organization. Responsiveness to mission and adaptability to environmental change is at the top of the triangle. Productivity is at the four-o'clock position—how well the mission is accomplished will determine the organization's long-run health. The pressure to do more with less is nearly always present. Quality of work life is at eight o'clock—doing the job well over the long haul depends on employee commitment and morale.

How are these things accomplished? The traditional answer has been

---

TABLE 6
What Is Expected of an Organization?

Responsive to mission and
adaptive to environment

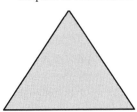

Quality of work life:
commitment, morale,
meaning

Productivity:
quantity, quality, cost
(do more with less)

found within the patriarchal strategy. The best answer, however, is *empowerment.*

The patriarchal strategy concentrates responsibility and leadership at the top and stresses belief in consistency, control, and predictability. The organization tells the employee "Do as I say and I will take care of you." The implicit patriarchal contract is to submit to authority, to deny self-expression, and to sacrifice now for often unstated promises—all in return for being "taken care of." Employees are instruments, tools to be controlled and prevented from diverting resources. The limits of the patriarchal strategy are that it alienates the doing of work from the managing of work, values internal stability for its own sake, encourages narrow functional thinking, limits ownership of plans and ideas, and breeds caution and resistance to change. Over time, employees feel betrayed if rewards are not forthcoming at the level they have grown to expect. The patriarchal strategy tends to produce victims who become envious of victors to the detriment of teamwork and productivity. The balance of forces tends to favor the status quo and to actively inhibit behavior that deviates from it—even if that behavior stands a good chance of furthering the vision.

The empowerment strategy, on the other hand, strives for commitment and leadership at every level and stresses diversity, innovation, and personal responsibility. The organization tells the employee, "We will support autonomy and choice." The empowerment contract is to accept your own authority and accountability, encourage straight communication, and make commitments based on their meaning—not how they may look to the boss. Setbacks are taken at face value rather than as an excuse for feeling like a victim. The value of empowerment is that people will think of the whole organization rather than think in narrow functional or personal terms. The empowered organization values change, so things don't have to be "broke" before they can be improved. (Remember, though, that the improvements should be in implementation quality and not necessarily design quality.) Empowerment allows unique responses as situations demand, with no need to wait for multiple levels of approval or instructions from higher authority. Finally, empowerment integrates the doing of work and the management of work with substantial dividends for productivity.

Employees must empower themselves, though the organization plays a critical role in removing barriers and providing encouragement. In the final analysis, the empowered employee will be strong enough and free enough to decide whether to accept a setback with continued commitment or decline to participate further. The decision to exit may take the form of changing employment or simply hunkering down and riding out the storm—in effect returning to the patriarchal model. This option is always present, and it provides leaders with the continuing challenge of keeping the environment for empowerment green.

Empowerment is not designed solely or even mainly to make people happy. The empowered organization is not "easy," but it does tend to have good morale. The tasks may be demanding, and meaning may be achieved only with great difficulty. Integrity means sailing under your own colors and having the strength to say no (not maybe) when you mean no. This can test relations with others, but contrast it with supervision by intimidation. Browbeating employees and ignoring their wants and needs may give the supervisor a sense of personal power, but that style alienates people and destroys productivity. A friend who is CEO of a major corporation says that while trying to have a positive impact on people is intrinsically gratifying and good, a sufficient reason for acting that way is that it works—it furthers the objectives of the organization. To paraphrase a quote attributed to noted author and former Secretary of the U.S. Department of Health, Education, and Welfare John Gardner, morale is not necessarily happy people and smiling faces. Rather, it is people believing that the organization and its leaders are going in the right direction and doing the right things. For higher education in these times, an important and visible component of the right thing must be to maximize the productivity of administration and support services.

THE ACTION PLAN

Imagine that the diagnoses have been completed and that the necessary preconditions for a successful productivity improvement program have been put in place. The momentum of cost-plus pricing has been arrested, and firm resource constraints have been installed. What specific action steps should be undertaken to channel these positive forces toward administration and support-service productivity improvement?

Communications

The first step is to develop a communications strategy. Wide understanding of the reasons why productivity should be high on the institution's agenda is essential for mounting an effective program. Change itself can be painful, and increased productivity requires firm limits on resource outlays in the face of demands for improved performance. Active participation requires that people understand why they are being asked to endure what may well seem like sacrifices.

But communication should be a two-way street. Creating a shared strategic vision requires listening carefully to what people at all levels of the organization are saying even though in the end the vision is heavily conditioned by the outside environment and determined by the leadership. Changes in the outside environment may best be interpreted by people on the firing line, and the overall vision must relate meaningfully to their goals and sense of reality. Genuine two-way communication is much easier in the empowered organization where one does not have to resort to patriarchal games and the adjudication of claims of victimhood. It is possible for a leader to listen carefully and in good faith to employees without abdicating the responsibility to set the organization's agenda. However, a true leader must be willing to explain a final decision but must not feel compelled to *prove* that it will be the right decision. (Such a burden is impossible. Leaders must be empowered to act on their own judgment, provided they are prepared to be held accountable.)

The communication process can take many forms. Management retreats are popular and they can be very effective. "Town meetings" where leaders meet with middle managers and rank-and-file employees can serve the dual purpose of generating a dialogue between top management and these other groups and facilitating communication among them. Management by walking around is another effective way of communicating.

While every situation is different, it is often a good idea to decide on the broad outlines of the vision in a small group setting before taking it on the road. The small group must include senior management, who must ultimately be responsible for vision content, though others who have taken the time to become expert in the issues can also play an important role. The vision is then refined by give-and-take exposure to broader groups. Finally, the basic content of the message is finalized and promulgated as widely as possible.

Video and other technical aids can be helpful in putting out a coherent and consistent message, since the time and energy of the most senior people—who have the greatest source credibility—is limited. However, there is no substitute for personal involvement. One useful format is for the CEO to videotape a message that is then played before a group in his or her presence, after which there is a discussion and questions session. This conserves the CEO's energy, guarantees the consistency of the message from session to session, and makes it possible for the CEO to think about the group during presentation of the core material.

Management Process

The productivity improvement program will not succeed without a well-thought-out management process for maintaining its place on the organization's agenda and keeping it on track. Experience suggests that the best method is to charge a high-level management group (a steering committee) with this task and then support it with a small staff that will be responsible for planning and follow-through. Keeping the program on the senior people's agenda despite inevitable distractions is a key responsibility for the staff. So is setting reasonably sized specific tasks, making appropriate delegations (with the support of the program's principals), and tracking the delegations to ensure performance. Since facilitating empowerment is a major goal, the staff must avoid the temptation to perform most of the tasks themselves. That would disempower line managers and ultimately undermine the program. One way to make sure this doesn't happen is for the senior people to keep the support staff very small, which would require it to go out into the organization to get things done. This also helps hold the line on task accretion by the staff group.

The usual way to go out into the organization is to delegate particular tasks to individuals or small groups, usually representative managers or staff with specifically relevant expertise. However, one of the lessons of the quality, service, and productivity (QSP) program my colleagues and I developed for Stanford's business and finance division was that an analog to quality circles can be very effective both in solving particular problems and facilitating empowerment. The variant we used was the quality team (we called them QSP teams), a format developed by the Hewlett-Packard Corporation. The team roster was constructed as a diagonal section through the organization, from top to bottom and from side to side. (The traditional quality circle is made up of bottom-level people—e.g., those on the factory floor.) The advantage is breadth of experience plus the ability of the few expert and higher-level participants to get information, assess the implementation possibilities of the group's ideas, and help get things done when the time comes. It is important, however, that these higher-level people consider themselves more as facilitators than as managers, lest the insight and energy of the others be stifled through disempowerment.

The steering committee's role in all this is to help conceptualize the process, set priorities for what tasks need to be attended to, and oversee the work of the staff. Another very important role is to provide an audience to which the work product of the task groups will ultimately be presented. In addition to its obvious value, such a role provides the task groups with a focal point for organizing themselves and a sense of recognition or even reward when they have accomplished their charge. Constructively critical questions from senior managers are in fact a powerful kind of recognition—one of the most powerful a motivated professional can achieve. Furthermore, the presentation sessions provide members of the steering committee with an opportunity to interact with employees from levels they would not usually have contact with and to do so in relation to a problem of mutual importance. We found that the QSP teams facilitate two-way communication and provide opportunities for senior managers to send signals about style and what they think is important.

Analysis and Planning

There is, of course, no substitute for having well-conceptualized and well-thought-out strategies and plans. They deal with the what and how of change, and they must be rooted in the objectively real world as well as in peoples' sense of subjective reality. For instance, computer systems that cannot work as envisioned because of technological limitations or because they require too much time or money to develop will not be helpful no matter how well they fit in with the vision and people's beliefs about what is important. Engineering, financial, market, contractual, legal, and regulatory factors have to be analyzed in depth in order to see possibilities and avoid mistakes. This kind of fact finding and analysis is part of the content of the delegations and charges to teams referred to in the previous section.

For example, an early action in Stanford's QSP program was to charge a team with trying to understand the elements of good service—what it means, how to get it, how to keep it. The team began the task by doing a systematic literature survey and then decided to talk with a number of companies identified as exemplary service providers. Out of this came some general principles: service must be a major organizational commitment (part of the vision, such as productivity must be); people must be trained in how to provide it, empowered to do so, and then held accountable for following through; and client feedback must be collected, as it is essential to understanding how things are going and to making midcourse corrections.

Eventually, what was learned by this team was embodied in the service training program discussed in connection with Table 5.

The QSP team on work simplification provides another example. It started by developing a definition and understanding of what is meant by work simplification. This led to the creation of two subteams for doing pilot studies of how Stanford hires and pays people and how Stanford buys things (that is, employment/payroll and procurement/accounts payable). One of their first tasks was to learn about work process flowcharting and then apply it in their own departments. Some of these people discovered they could actually change the way the work was being done. The most spectacular result was in accounts payable, where a change in work flow and procedures reduced the backlog and the use of overtime to virtually nothing while coping with increased transaction volume and maintaining a constant staff—something the finance division had been trying to do for years without success. The final lesson was that much could be accomplished when the people with an intimate knowledge of the process were motivated and empowered to change it and given the tools to do so.

Rewards, Recognition, and Incentives

The "Welcome" section of the Stanford controller's office *RR&I Handbook* begins: "Tom Peters, author of *A Passion for Excellence,* has said that employees come to work equipped with motivation. The manager's job, therefore, is not to motivate, but to capitalize on the resource that is already there by removing minor barriers and constantly recognizing small achievements." The handbook goes on to state: "To be most effective, such recognition must be spontaneous and ongoing. By taking individual responsibility for recognizing our colleagues' daily efforts, we can achieve a culture where recognition is second nature and the incentive to excel accompanies each new task." The *Handbook* presents "simple, straightforward guidelines for recognizing and rewarding day-to-day efforts," some of which are reproduced in Table 7, which appears on the next page. What is particularly impressive is that the guidelines were developed by the line managers themselves rather than by human resource professionals—a tangible example of empowerment.

The more traditional processes of performance evaluations and merit pay should not be overlooked in designing RR&I systems. Written performance evaluations are tremendously important and well worth spending time on. Many organizations, including Stanford, have well-developed processes, including packaged materials and training programs on how to use them. I have found it helpful to ask for a sample of six to twelve of the evaluations written by people who report to me or by those a level lower, who report to them. I do this a month or two after the official performance-evaluation season has ended, partly to look at the performance of the evaluated, partly to see whether the evaluator is doing the job conscientiously, and partly to send a signal that I care about the process. With regard to merit pay, the biggest problem is how to increase the range of variation from a point or two from the guideline to as much as two times it. There is no sure way to do this within traditional merit pay systems, though a process wherein senior managers reject packages with unusually small ranges would certainly be a step in the right direction.

TABLE 7
Criteria and Suggestions for Individual and Team Rewards.

Criteria (typical examples of an employee's willingness to go the extra mile)	*Rewards (to be used as a menu of rewards and as a catalyst for new ideas)*
• Suggested/developed a system or process that improved the quality, service, and/or productivity of work.	• Recognition party or dinner.
• Suggested/developed a system or process for work-simplification.	• Lunch at Stanford Faculty Club.
• Developed a creative solution to meet the needs of a client or department.	• Permission to attend seminars, workshops, and classes outside of university staff development classes.
• Assumed additional responsibilities during a period of staff shortage.	• Tickets for two to Stanford events such as Lively Arts performances and athletics events.
• Increased job knowledge by voluntarily participating in cross training.	• Attendance at special lectures, presentations, or other university events.
• Exhibited tact and diplomacy in dealing with faculty, staff, or the outside community on a sensitive issue beyond the normal scope of job.	• Behind-the-scenes tour (perhaps with family) of Stanford facilities such as the linear accelerator, the biological preserve, the marine station, or the hospital.
• Made a difficult decision by using sound judgment and reasoning and carefully weighing alternatives.	• A gift from the Stanford bookstore, track house, or art gallery shop.
• Consistently promoting teamwork by help and cooperation outside of requirements.	• Personalized office supplies (pen, etc.).
	• A handwritten thank-you note.

From the *Rewards, Recognition, and Incentives Handbook* produced by the Stanford University controller's office.

Finally, one might consider a nontraditional program of providing merit salary increments not in the base. The idea is that the half or two-thirds of employees who are doing the best job are given salary increments averaging several percent, but these increments would not be added to the person's base salary for compounding in future years. The increment would keep coming as long as performance held up, but it would not be guaranteed. It would be awarded in addition to the normal compounding increments received by everyone, which in the experiment become simple market adjustments. The program is intended to stretch the range of annual merit variations while avoiding the problem of consistently good or bad performance compounding to greater-than-tolerable disparities. The system would be calibrated so that people who don't get the nonbase increment would be slightly below market while those who got the best increments would be above market.

Measurement

The idea of measurement has permeated much of what I have said about productivity improvement. There are a number of reasons for this. First, no system can function effectively without feedback. The ability to assess the gap between performance and expectations is fundamental to midcourse correction, and no one is smart enough or well-informed enough to create a plan that can work without such corrections. Second, rewards, recognition, and incentives require that someone, somehow, makes an assessment of whether work is good, bad, or indifferent. It works the other way too, of course: accountability requires that an assessment be made of results.

I have already discussed one aspect of measurement in connection with communication. Two-way communication is a form of measurement: What's on your mind and how are we, the management, doing? A friend suggested that the way to approach this kind of measurement is to ask, "If I could sit on a bar stool with everyone in the organization for an hour, what would I suggest we talk about?" One way to do that (other than logging many hours on bar stools) is to hold town meetings and insist on candor in the ensuing discussions. Another is to use impromptu written surveys during town meetings, management retreats, and similar functions. The questionnaire does not need to be elaborate, though a degree of consistency will permit comparisons to be made across groups and over time. Sometimes the answers can be tabulated and feedback provided to the group at the same meeting. This usually guarantees that the question-and-answer period will be candid and lively.

Constantly taking the pulse of the organization is one of the keys of effective management. The same is true of client feedback. One of the things the QSP team learned about successful service organizations was that they all go out of their way to obtain systematic feedback from clients and then act on it promptly. The process of acquiring and paying attention to feedback is built into the organization's culture. It is part of its vision and part of its performance evaluation criteria. Experience shows that acting on feedback improves results. Measurement of how productivity improvement is being achieved has to be an integral part of any program.

What feedback is likely to be important in a productivity program? First, there needs to be a systematic attempt to chronicle the specific actions being taken to support the program: what decisions, initiatives, investments, resource reallocations, and work simplification projects are being attempted and what their results are. Sometimes self-assessment is the best or most practical method of evaluation; sometimes it should be done by superiors and sometimes by staff groups, outside consultants, or visiting committees. Whatever the method, the important thing is that there be a description of the action, an a priori statement of the expected outcomes, and an explicit evaluation. The objective is both to learn by doing and to keep score for purposes of RR&I and accountability—the latter being based on the willingness to intelligently act as well as on the efficacy of the final outcome.

The other kind of measure is to keep score on the aggregate performance of operating units with respect to productivity measures. Where the inputs and outputs can be reasonably quantified, the score keeping should be straightforward. Transactions processed per FTE employee is a natural measure in the general accounting department, for instance. Lacking quantification of this sort, it may still be possible to track the number of employees that perform various qualitatively described tasks. It often is possible to measure performance on the basis of budget reallocation that the unit undertakes. Most organizations operate in a dynamic environment, and a long period of organizational stability may well signal a failure to adapt to new requirements or challenges and a stagnation of productivity improvement.

The bottom line is that the organization will tend to pay attention to the things that are posted on the scoreboard—provided, of course, that management makes clear that it is looking at the scoreboard too. The design of a productivity program must include output measures to assess how the program is going. Those measures need to be assessed at the operating unit level where people are close enough to the action to make a difference.

A POSTSCRIPT ON MANAGEMENT STYLE

There is no magic potion for productivity improvement in colleges and universities. Even when dealing with administrative and support services, the obstacles are large and the gains hard won. No large-scale purchase of capital equipment will make the difference. Even when information technology supplants manual processes, the gains are achieved little by little. Small wins by people newly empowered and eager to make a difference are what add up to the final result. The challenge of leadership is to see that the battles are fought on the right ground and for the right objectives; to recognize, reward, and hold people accountable so that the process continues and gains momentum; and to enable people to achieve these wins.

It is a truism that top managers must wholeheartedly support the program, making it a sine qua non for the organization, if there is to be real success. Their attitude must be positive, and they must be willing to shoulder risks both for the organization and for themselves. There should be a bias toward action, an approach that says "try it, fix it" rather than "study it until we're sure it'll work" or "discuss it until we have consensus."

The members of the management team must learn to work together and, above all, must trust one another. Each must carry the others' proxy—to get things done for the good of the organization, they must recognize transgressions and fix them when they occur rather than play "one up." The management team must "zig and zag together," in the words of William F. Miller, former provost of Stanford University and president of SRI International, a nonprofit research institute based in Menlo Park, California. Each member of the team must anticipate what the other will do and make maximum use of that knowledge to get the job done. Not only is this a necessary condition for performing the senior group's tasks effectively but it sets an important example for the rest of the organization. And it applies across the boundary between academic and administrative units as well as within the culture of each.

Finally, it may be useful to initially present the productivity-improvement task as removing impediments rather than as instituting an ideal system all at once. All organizations abound with impediments, and this is especially true of many colleges and universities. Creating the right vision and getting back to neutral on productivity by eliminating redun-

dancy; controlling the cost of quality; or progressing toward work simplification, empowerment, and RR&I represent good initial goals. After a few
years, the goal should be to make the whole greater than the sum of the parts
through better coordination of functions and global optimization of capital
and human resource investments. This is an exciting process. When higher
education has mastered it, it shall no longer have to be on the defensive with
respect to productivity—the public and the political system will recognize
higher education's productivity when they see it.

Bibliography

Association of American Universities Ad Hoc Committee on Indirect Costs. *Indirect Costs Associated with Federal Support of Research on University Campuses: Some Suggestions for Change.* Washington: Association of American Universities, 1988.

Allen, Richard, and Paul Brinkman. *Marginal Costing Techniques for Higher Education.* Boulder: National Center for Higher Education Management Systems (NCHEMS), 1983.

Barney, Jay B., and William G. Ouchi. *Organizational Economics.* San Francisco: Jossey-Bass Publishers, 1986.

Baumol, William J., and Sue Anne Batey Blackman. "Electronics, the Cost Disease, and the Operation of Libraries." *Journal of the American Society for Information Sciences,* vol. 34 (3): 181–91.

Block, Peter. *The Empowered Manager.* San Francisco: Jossey-Bass Publishers, 1988.

Bowen, William. *The Economics of the Major Private Universities.* New York: Carnegie Commission on Higher Education, 1968.

Davis, Stanley M. *Future Perfect.* Reading, Mass.: Addison-Wesley Publishing Company, 1987.

Finn, Chester E., Jr. "Judgment Time for Higher Education: In the Court of Public Opinion." *Change,* vol. 20:34–39.

Hannaway, Jane. "Supply Creates Demands: An Organizational Process View of Administrative Expansion." *Journal of Policy Analysis and Management,* vol. 7:118–34.

Hauptman, Arthur M. "Why Are College Charges Increasing? Looking Into the Various Explanations." Working draft of a report to the College Board and the American Council of Education, September 1988.

Heskett, James L. "Lessons from the Service Sector." *Harvard Business Review,* (March-April 1987): 118-26.

Hoenack, Stephen A. *Economic Behavior Within Organizations.* New York: Cambridge University Press, 1983.

Maister, David H. "Professional Service Firm Management." Memo no. 20. Boston: Harvard Business School (June 1984).

March, James G. "Emerging Developments in the Study of Organizations." *Review of Higher Education,* vol. 6 (1982): 1–18.

Massy, William F. "Productivity and Cost Increase at Stanford." Discussion paper no. 2. Stanford University Board of Trustees Budget Committee (7 May 1984).

————. "Financing Higher Education." Tenth annual conference on financing higher education. National Center for Higher Education Management Systems (NCHEMS) (28 November 1984).

————. "Strategies for Productivity Improvement in College and University Academic Departments." Presented at the Forum for Postsecondary Governance, 30 October 1989, Santa Fe, New Mexico.

Meyer, Marshall W. *Limits to Bureaucratic Growth.* Berlin: Walter de Gruyter, 1985.

Pfeffer, Jeffrey, and Gerald R. Salancik. *The External Control of Organizations: A Recourse Dependence Perspective.* New York: Harper & Row, Publishers, 1978.

The Higher Education Research Program (Sponsored by the Pew Charitable Trusts), "Double Trouble." *Policy Perspectives,* vol. 2, no. 1 (September 1989).

Simon, Herbert A. "The Steam Engine and the Computer: What Makes Technology Revolutionary." *EDUCOM Bulletin,* vol. 22, no. 1 (Spring 1987): 2–5.

Sullivan, Charles Parker. "The Social Construction of Change in Administrative Behavior in Higher Education." Ph.D. diss., Stanford University, 1987.

Weber, Max. "Types of Legitimate Domination." *Economy and Society,* vol. 1. Guenther Roth and Claus Wittick, eds. 212–301. Berkeley: University of California Press, 1978.

Weick, Karl E. "Small Wins: Redefining the Scale of Social problems." *American Psychologist,* vol. 39, no. 1 (1984): 40–49.

Chapter 4

Achieving Productivity Gains in Financial Management

George R. Houston Jr.

Senior Vice President and Treasurer
Georgetown University

Although colleges and universities are increasingly concerned with improving their overall productivity, few have developed ways in which such gains can be effectively demonstrated. In this chapter, a university's chief financial officer explains the critical importance of documenting improvements in financial management and shows how his department instituted the processes necessary to achieve this goal.

Productivity can be defined as "producing abundantly" or "increasing effective results." Where the higher education community has fallen short is in its failure to adequately *demonstrate* increased effective results. Watch disbelief creep across trustees' faces when they learn that the normal teaching load is not six hours per day but six hours per week! Does this mean we are less productive with a six-hour teaching load than when we had a nine- or even twelve-hour load? Most academics would answer "no" and explain that a greater amount of nonteaching time is being devoted to research. Yet few have effectively demonstrated how their research has improved the quality of—or productivity in—academic life.

In addition to being a university vice president, I am trained as an accountant. This profession has been a great asset to academia in helping it meet the ever-growing number of fiscal regulations instituted by federal, state, and local governments and various organizations responsible for establishing standardized accounting principles. Where the accounting profession has failed to assist academia, however, is in developing ways to document productivity gains. Such certification may be more critical to the long-term financial health of higher education institutions than the fact that our financial statements conform with some group's generally accepted accounting standards.

Setting this important issue aside for the moment, I want to examine productivity from the perspective of an institution's chief financial officer (CFO) and to show how productivity gains can be achieved as part of the management of an institution's financial affairs.

THE ROLES OF THE CFO

In an academic enterprise, the chief financial officer's mission is to provide needed services in a personable, cost-efficient, dependable, and timely fashion, enabling the university to meet its teaching, research, and public service goals. If this mission is fulfilled successfully, improved productivity on an institution-wide scale should follow. As such, a university CFO has four major roles to play: goal setter, developer of policy, monitor of policy effectiveness, and interpreter of financial information for others.

Goal Setter

The CFO should *participate* in developing institutional goals. This is an inclusive, not exclusive, exercise: Collegiality must preside if long-term peace and commitment are to prevail. The CFO's function is to provide data, ask difficult questions, and suggest alternatives. Final decisions must be made by all the goal setters, of which the CFO is only one. Surely emergencies will arise when everyone cannot be consulted, but these should be exceptions and not the rule.

Compared to the academic, student affairs, or health delivery representatives, the CFO's responsibility as an institutional representative is to get everyone to focus on the big picture. It is easy to balance the books by deferring maintenance, but it is also true that buildings cannot repair themselves—sooner or later a price will have to be paid for such practices. My personal experience suggests that getting individuals who are involved in the planning process focused is the most delicate part of the job and requires great diplomatic skills.

Developer of Policy

Once institutional goals have been established, the CFO should issue the necessary financial policies and procedures. This aspect of the job should be viewed as implementing the collegially established institutional goals or meeting external requirements (i.e., federal and state regulations).

Monitor of Policy Effectiveness

Accurate, timely reporting on the progress made toward meeting goals is essential. One of the most important functions of a financial officer is the design and implementation of reporting systems. Once there is the perception—right or wrong—that reports are incorrect, incoherent, or outdated, it will take tremendous time and effort to overcome. Effort should be spent on making reports, policies, and procedures understandable to the laity.

For example, Georgetown's financial policies and procedures are contained in the *Financial Information Systems Handbook* (FISH). Each summer this handbook is revised by a student editor. This person collects policy and procedure revisions from operating departments, edits text changes, and publishes the revisions. The editor, who has no financial background, provides a check on the clarity of the guidelines.

Interpreter of Financial Information

University financial statements are not the easiest reports to understand. Several years ago, a trustee with twelve years on the board expressed amazement at how Georgetown's equity had grown while the school maintained a balanced budget. He had ignored increases in the endowment and in loan and plant funds and had looked only at current funds. A similar lack of perception of the whole picture is found among other constituents, not the least of whom are faculty, students, and alumni. I am a firm believer that if you effectively communicate your story—be it financial or other—people will respond positively. For years now I have prepared a consolidated balance sheet and a consolidated statement of changes in fund balances to communicate key financial data. Similarly, one issue of the alumni magazine is devoted exclusively to Georgetown's annual report.

The higher education community must do a better job of explaining cost increases. The press is constantly comparing changes in educational costs with changes in the Consumer Price Index (CPI). Meanwhile, the federal government frequently discusses limiting indirect cost recovery on grants and contracts. At least one proposal has been made to reduce federal financial aid funds by the amount of tuition increases in excess of the CPI. All of this highlights the need for a better explanation of costing policies.

TOOLS OF THE TRADE

In addition to helping the university achieve greater productivity institution-wide (admittedly, a task that could occupy a major segment of any administrator's time), the CFO must work to improve the productivity of the financial office—and in so doing point the way toward more productive practices for other areas of the university. Complementing the four primary roles of the CFO are three primary means through which long- and short-term results can be accomplished: goal setting, budgeting, and effective communication.

Goal Setting

Since their founding, business schools have taught planning or goal setting as a management function. Yet when it comes to practicing what we preach, higher education has found it not so easy.

Years ago I questioned an academic administrator on his goals for the next five years. His answer? He had not given it any thought. I countered that at least he would not be disappointed when he got there, since he did not know where "there" was. My message got through. With my help, he soon commenced long-range (five year) planning. Plans of this sort are essential. They force an entire university to focus on the future.

Goal setting should permeate the entire enterprise and should not be limited to the institutional level. It is just as essential at departmental and employee levels in order to achieve motivation, planning, delegation, coordination, and control.

Motivation. Everyone needs a sense of accomplishment. Without defined goals, how will people know if they have accomplished anything? More important, how can they know if what they accomplished is recognized by peers and superiors? Meeting established goals fulfills a basic need.

Planning. The pyramiding of individual goals can produce some very effective institutional plans. A clear definition of individual goals encourages unified planning. When the new president of Georgetown was appointed, a committee was formed to prepare a briefing book for him. So many people working on a common objective had a unifying effect.

Delegation. Hiring good people, defining their responsibilities, and turning them loose can result in total chaos. For delegation to be effective, common goals must be accepted.

Coordination. I have frequently compared my role as CFO to the conductor of an orchestra. While I cannot play every instrument, I must coordinate the tune that is being played and the tempo at which it is played and make certain that every instrument is playing its part and has its turn in the spotlight. Otherwise our symphony, financial affairs, will not be in harmony.

Control. Meaningful control requires defining results. This is the basis for a clear understanding of what constitutes good performance. The completion of agreed-upon goals speaks to good performance and should be considered in evaluations and promotions.

For several years I have met quarterly with the financial affairs staff to discuss goals. These meetings have gone through an evolutionary process. Originally, only the senior staff met; now there are twenty-three managers who participate. The meetings keep us informed of each division's progress, problems, schedules for new studies, and systems of operating. On more than one occasion as a result of these meetings, plans have been altered to coordinate the activities of multiple divisions. The meetings used to last an entire day. Now they take only a half day. A shorter meeting with more participants was achieved by having each division submit a written report on the status of the previous quarter's goals—accomplished, still in process, postponed, or discontinued—along with a preview of the next quarter's goals. These reports are distributed to the participants a few days before the meeting.

In order to focus on major activities, only three or four goals are submitted by each division (administration, budget, cashiers, controller, cost accounting, sponsored programs, and treasury) per meeting. Each goal identifies tasks that need to be performed, resources needed, and measurement criteria. For example, one of the controller's goals for the first quarter of fiscal year 1990 was the completion of the fiscal year 1989 audit one month earlier than the previous year. That goal's measurement was a date.

Goal setting at the departmental and employee levels is important for team building. Each employee is asked by his or her supervisor what personal goals or objectives are on the agenda for the next quarter. An accounts payable employee's goal might be to eliminate any backlog in remitting invoices or to pay all of them within a certain number of days. Individual goals are then consolidated at the departmental and divisional levels and discussed at the quarterly meeting. This process has helped us improve productivity on both the individual and departmental levels: the entire staff has a better understanding of what tune we are playing and when, where, and why we are playing it.

This was not accomplished overnight. It took patience and persistence, and the system is still being improved. When I announced that annual merit reviews would consider goal setting and achievements, more attention was paid to the quarterly meetings. Goals became more realistic and failures occurred less often. We are becoming better planners, better managers.

Budgeting Process

Another way in which a university can increase productivity is in the preparation of its annual budget. Georgetown's total budget is over a half-billion dollars and has been balanced for nineteen consecutive years. Naturally, this involves carefully coordinating and directing many people—a function of the Budget Advisory Committee (BAC), which advises the president. The BAC's voting membership includes the vice president for financial affairs who is the chairman, the executive vice president for the main campus, the executive vice president for health sciences, the executive vice president for the law center, and the vice president for planning, but all of the university's vice presidents of administration and facilities, alumni and university relations, campus ministries, and urban affairs participate in BAC meetings.

Georgetown has used a three-campus budget process for fifteen years. It requires each of the three academic campuses—main, medical, and law (plus the auxiliary enterprises associated with each)—to prepare and maintain balanced budgets. Each area's budget includes overhead costs for operations and maintenance, alumni and university relations, student services, and general administration. The BAC annually reviews the methods of allocating overhead for fairness. Once agreement on allocation methods is reached, a call is issued for departments to submit requests for the next fiscal year. These requests are summarized and distributed to the BAC for review at its September meeting. Simultaneously with the overhead reviews, campus budget committees commence their deliberations in order to make preliminary projections at the fall board of trustees meeting on such subjects as the general inflation level, faculty and staff salary increases, tuition increases, and enrollment projections.

After receiving preliminary board approval, the campuses finalize their plans, which are then consolidated into the *University Financial Plan* and presented to the president for approval. The *Plan* is also mailed to the board of trustees at least two weeks prior to its March meeting. Following the board's final approval, the budget office issues the requisite forms to enter line-item budgets into the accounting and budgeting system. The entire process takes one year.

One of the advantages of Georgetown's three-campus budget model is

Georgetown's Budget Calendar

June	Budget Advisory Committee reviews allocation methods
July	Overhead budget call issued by the budget office
August	Overhead budget requests due to the budget office
September	BAC initial review of overhead requests and preliminary planning parameters delivered to the board of trustees
November	BAC approves final overhead requests
January	Campus plans finalized
February	Campus plans due to the budget office
	Presidential review of the *University Financial Plan*
March	*Plan* approved by the board of trustees
April	Budget office issues line-item budget call
May	Budgets due to the budget office
June	Budget office reconciles line-item budgets with *Plan* while the BAC reviews allocation methods in preparation for the new budget year

that each major division is responsible for not only developing but also maintaining a balanced budget. At the end of the year, the BAC meets to discuss variances from the budget. At that time, requests are received for one-time expenditures, transfers to endowment, unexpended plant funds, and other restricted accounts to fund future programs. If deficits occur, previously accumulated reserves may be liquidated.

Does the three-campus model work? Most people at Georgetown would say it does. Two examples demonstrate its success. A number of years ago, the Law Center Budget Committee established as its first priority library book purchases, not faculty salaries. Only a faculty committee could recommend such a priority shift. If the president or the CFO had made such a proposal, it would not have been accepted. More recently, the Medical School Finance Committee recommended that the faculty adopt a process of taxation to raise seed money for new programs in its division. This course of action was adopted. Recommendations of these kinds are much more palatable if they come from the faculties directly affected.

Effective Communication

With the amount of information needed to keep each campus and division informed, communication is a major challenge. The use of computers in this role is not new, and an increasingly popular computer-based communication technique is electronic mail.

Electronic mail has been a real timesaver at Georgetown. How many times have you played telephone tag with your president, provost, or other officers? Many of those calls are simple questions that require simple answers. Our electronic mail system has reduced the number of calls, returned calls, and returns of returned calls. It is an excellent communications tool with multiple uses. With it, we can track who is in or out of the office so everyone knows who has signature authority on a particular day and when that person can be reached. We hope to refine this system so that we can eventually schedule meetings without having to use the telephone.

When we decided to install an electronic mail system the fear on the faces of the fiscal staff was a sight to see. I hired an English major/computer science minor who had worked with us during his undergraduate years as technology assistant and turned him loose to teach the staff how to use the system. He was an instant success. At minimal cost, everyone was provided with a nonthreatening, private tutor. Today the technology assistant is installing local area networks and initiating a pilot program in optical storage. The financial affairs staff sees his hiring as one of my best decisions. It is usually productive to look in-house and see what talent is available. Do not overlook your graduate and undergraduate business students. They are usually hungry for some hands-on experience for a class project. My experience with them has been great.

SUMMARY

These are just a few examples of how a two-hundred-year-old university has changed to become more productive. Increased productivity is easy to document in the financial area. More invoices are processed, more bills are paid, and more accounts are managed with the same or smaller staffs. However, that does not answer the larger question—has the entire enterprise become more productive?

Looking at the scientific sides of the academies, the answer is affirmative. Research conducted in medical schools has demonstrably increased effective results in the health sciences. At the turn of the century, medical students were being trained to diagnose cardiac conditions. By the 1960s, they were learning procedures to replace defective or diseased heart valves. Today, complicated by-pass operations are somewhat routine and heart transplant have prolonged the lives of thousands of individuals. Everyone agrees that, over a relatively short span of one hundred years, medical research has been increasingly productive.

But other aspects of higher education need to demonstrate productivity gains as well. Undergraduates are constantly implored to reflect and meditate on the higher values that are presumably cultivated by a university education. But how are reflection and meditation measured? What do they produce? Time must be devoted to these questions.

Chapter 5

Increasing Productivity in Facilities Management

Harvey H. Kaiser

Senior Vice President, Facilities Administration
Syracuse University

At almost every institution, facilities maintenance is among the areas
that present the greatest opportunities for productivity improvement. Effective maintenance management can be achieved only through ongoing analysis of the systems that make up the overall operation. Harvey
Kaiser addresses the importance of assessing a system's efficiency and
outlines a procedure whereby managers can evaluate the effectiveness
of their own maintenance organization.

Administrators faced with the mandate to improve productivity campuswide are taking a hard look at the efficiency and effectiveness of maintenance management. A massive backlog of deferred maintenance, the expense of renewing and replacing deteriorated physical plants, and the
demand to reduce budgets require assurances that current operations are being conducted as efficiently as possible. This chapter describes a process for
analyzing the efficiency and effectiveness of maintenance management in
identifying problem areas that need immediate attention and opportunities
for further study.

The benefits of increasing the productivity of building maintenance
management are both quantitative and qualitative. A more productive labor
force is more efficient and more effective and results in more work of a

The author acknowledges use in this chapter of material published in *The Maintenance
Management Audit* (R. S. Means Company, Inc., 1991). The subject was developed in
cooperation with Applied Management Engineering of Virginia Beach, Va., and the
assistance of William Thomas.

higher quality being done. The improved performance of the labor force is apparent in facilities improvements and, as such, becomes visible to the entire campus community, which can sense the higher level of morale and pride among the laborers.

Typically, building maintenance represents 30 to 36 percent of an institution's operations and maintenance budget; it is the area where the greatest opportunities for increased productivity exist. Analyses of maintenance expenditures undertaken by various types of higher education institutions (research, comprehensive, two-year, etc.) to measure productivity have a common thread—they all deal with how a worker's time is spent.

A worker's day can be divided into three categories: direct productive (any work that contributes directly to altering the composition, condition, or construction of the item or area being repaired or altered); indirect productive (work that renders service for the productive portion of a job, such as planning); and nonproductive (idle or personal time spent by the worker).

Productivity is defined as the percentage of total hours spent on direct-productive activities. It can be measured with considerable accuracy by the statistical technique of work sampling. The results of studies conducted at a number of maintenance shops located at universities, military installations, and corporations indicate that productivity ranged between 38 and 48 percent, with an overall average of 43 percent. Optimum productivity is usually considered to range between 65 and 70 percent, but a reasonable initial target is 55 to 60 percent. With the optimum productivity level 70 percent and the average actual productivity 43 percent, the potential gain in those shops is 27 percent!

That this high level of potential for improvement exists appears to indicate a gross dereliction of duty by management, but without effective work-control procedures in place, low productivity is the norm.

MANAGEMENT INTERVENTION

Management intervention to enhance productivity and allow more resources to be returned to operations and maintenance is needed. In Chapter 1, William Massy describes such intervention as strategies that afford the possibility of mitigating or reversing inhibiting factors and unleashing forces that will enhance productivity. For example, a facilities management staff could be challenged to create productivity gains that would enable them to retain savings and keep the budget base intact for additional staff and materials. A primary benefit of this strategy would be the reallocation of funds to reduce deferred and backlogged maintenance and to improve and extend the life of facilities.

The two principal conditions that require management intervention are productivity-inhibiting situations and personnel problems associated with change. Productivity-inhibiting situations can come from the policies and procedures of an institution or from lack of aggressive leadership. Personnel problems are generally evidenced by foot-dragging, complaints about work requests, and unavailability of resources when new policies, procedures, or personnel are put in place. If a significant amount of work is being accomplished and an institution's budget is balanced, however, the motivation of management to increase productivity may be absent. Nevertheless, there are some readily apparent indicators that invite management intervention. These include backlogs of emergency, regular, and preventive maintenance; high levels of overtime; deferred maintenance; and emergency purchase orders.

The dilemma for administrators is how to determine whether or not intervention by the management team in charge of operations and maintenance will be effective. Administrators may chose to challenge the managers and provide some guidance for initiating productivity reviews, or they may seek assistance from outside consultants. Guidance may take the form of the maintenance management program review described in the subsequent section. Of course, "people problems" can come into play if a review is undertaken. If they do, administrators must decide either to support the management and use consultants to conduct the first-stage review or to make changes in personnel.

Assessing System Efficiency and Effectiveness

In structuring an assessment of maintenance management, efficiency and effectiveness can be measured by the following four factors.

- *Productivity*—the proportion of a worker's time that is directly productive.
- *Performance*—how well an individual works.
- *Quality*—the characteristics of the work product.
- *Priorities*—whether the priorities set by management are appropriate.

As a general rule, the better the maintenance management system, the more these four factors will be enhanced and the more effective the overall maintenance operation will be.

Undertaking a review of a maintenance management program is the first step in evaluating management effectiveness. The review is meant to answer the basic question: Are resources being put to the best possible use? If the framework for the review takes the form of an effectiveness rating summary, management activities can be analyzed in a systematic manner and a productivity improvement plan can be easily developed. A by-product of this process is that administrative practices and activities that require management attention can also be identified.

Once the broad improvement actions are culled from the review and implemented, the second step, a more detailed study using work sampling techniques to identify specific areas of potential productivity gains, can be started. To gauge the effectiveness of all of the resulting program changes, the entire process should be repeated every few years.

The Maintenance Management Program Review

The review approach focuses on the effectiveness of operations and maintenance programs. Factors common to maintenance management should be identified and a system for rating the degree of actual use and successful implementation should be developed. The process should be viewed as a preliminary review of maintenance management to identify general conditions and to note areas that need immediate attention. A complete review includes observation and measurement of the effectiveness of management, development of a productivity improvement action plan, implementation of systems improvements, and further evaluation and refinement of those systems. This process may also require the assistance of an outside consultant.

The first step of the program review is the management effectiveness analysis. The analysis should provide a program effectiveness rating, identification of problem areas where improvements are needed, and broad indication of potential gains. Once this part of the process is completed, the recommended improvements should be implemented. When the initial benefits from these improvements are achieved, the more detailed performance and work-quality problems that were identified should be corrected.

The process of observing and evaluating a maintenance management system will result in an overview of an entire program. By assigning a numerical effectiveness rating to the findings, areas that need immediate attention can be easily targeted. Such a rating also provides the yardstick against which future analyses can be measured.

Table 1 presents an effectiveness rating form that covers the five basic elements of maintenance management—organization, work load identification, work planning, work accomplishment, and appraisal—and the key components of each of them. The development of this suggested outline for an initial review is based on extensive experience managing maintenance

TABLE 1
Effectiveness Rating Summary.

	In Use	Fully Implemented	Total
ORGANIZATION			
Policies, rules	0 1 2 3	0 1 2 3	_____
Organization functions	0 1 2 3	0 1 2 3	_____
Work Control Center (functions)	0 1 2 3	0 1 2 3	_____
Work Control Center (staffing)	0 1 2 3	0 1 2 3	_____
Shop organization	0 1 2 3	0 1 2 3	_____
Shop supervisory and planning functions	0 1 2 3	0 1 2 3	_____
SUBTOTAL			_____
PERCENT			_____
WORK LOAD IDENTIFICATION			
Facilities inventory	0 1 2 3	0 1 2 3	_____
Facility condition inspection	0 1 2 3	0 1 2 3	_____
Work request procedure	0 1 2 3	0 1 2 3	_____
Equipment inventory	0 1 2 3	0 1 2 3	_____
Preventive maintenance	0 1 2 3	0 1 2 3	_____
Service work	0 1 2 3	0 1 2 3	_____
Routine recurring work	0 1 2 3	0 1 2 3	_____
Work requirements documentation	0 1 2 3	0 1 2 3	_____
SUBTOTAL			_____
PERCENT			_____
WORK PLANNING			
Priority criteria	0 1 2 3	0 1 2 3	_____
Work classification	0 1 2 3	0 1 2 3	_____
Alterations and improvement work approval	0 1 2 3	0 1 2 3	_____
Work-order preparation	0 1 2 3	0 1 2 3	_____
Budget requirements	0 1 2 3	0 1 2 3	_____
Backlogged deferred maintenance and repair	0 1 2 3	0 1 2 3	_____
Budget execution plan	0 1 2 3	0 1 2 3	_____
Backlogged funded work	0 1 2 3	0 1 2 3	_____
SUBTOTAL			_____
PERCENT			_____
WORK ACCOMPLISHMENTS			
Shop scheduling and planning procedure	0 1 2 3	0 1 2 3	_____
Craft and material availability	0 1 2 3	0 1 2 3	_____
Training program	0 1 2 3	0 1 2 3	_____
Shop spaces, tools, and equipment	0 1 2 3	0 1 2 3	_____
Storeroom operation	0 1 2 3	0 1 2 3	_____
Transportation	0 1 2 3	0 1 2 3	_____
Shop supervision	0 1 2 3	0 1 2 3	_____
Use of contracts	0 1 2 3	0 1 2 3	_____
SUBTOTAL			_____
PERCENT			_____
APPRAISAL			
Management information systems	0 1 2 3	0 1 2 3	_____
Performance measurement	0 1 2 3	0 1 2 3	_____
Productivity measurement	0 1 2 3	0 1 2 3	_____
Variance reviews	0 1 2 3	0 1 2 3	_____
Facility history records	0 1 2 3	0 1 2 3	_____
Equipment history records	0 1 2 3	0 1 2 3	_____
Trend data	0 1 2 3	0 1 2 3	_____
SUBTOTAL			_____
PERCENT			_____

organizations, undertaking consulting assignments, and reviewing maintenance management literature. If the form is to be used by an institution's staff or by consultants, it should be reviewed thoroughly, modified to meet the users' systems and language, and accompanied by a glossary of terms.

Evaluation procedure. When using an effectiveness rating form, the elements and indicators should be rated according to the following key: (0) not in place, (1) minimal, (2) partial, and (3) in place and appears effective.

In Table 2, the organization section of the form has been completed and the rating totals 24. The effectiveness rating of the organization of the management of this hypothetical maintenance program equals 24/36 (the largest total possible for this section), or 67 percent.

TABLE 2

ORGANIZATION	In Use	Fully Implemented	Total
Policies, rules	0 1 ②3	0 1 2 ③	5
Organization functions	0 1 2 ③	0 1 ②3	5
Work Control Center (functions)	0 1 ②3	0 1 ②3	4
Work Control Center (staffing)	0 1 ②3	0 ①2 3	3
Shop organization	0 1②3	0 1 ②3	4
Shop supervisory and planning functions	0 1②3	0 ①2 3	3
SUBTOTAL	13	11	24
PERCENT			24/36 = 67%

When each of the five basic elements has been evaluated, the scores are totaled and the average provides the overall effectiveness rating. A maintenance management program that has all indicators "in use" and "fully implemented" will achieve an excellent effectiveness rating. Experience has shown that there is a close correlation between program effectiveness and productivity—higher system effectiveness means higher productivity. For example, a program effectiveness rating of 40 percent would indicate the potential for considerable improvement. Forty percent is well below the initial productivity target range of 55 to 60 percent.

The objective is to define the system elements that can be improved to meet that target range. As the system effectiveness improves, the productivity level will also improve. The ultimate goal is to move the effectiveness rating to 75 percent.

Work Sampling

While a productivity improvement action plan can be based on the results of a program review, implementation of those targeted improvements may be followed by more extensive productivity analyses. By applying the statistical technique of work sampling, many specific factors that adversely affect the productivity of labor can be identified and quantified. Some adverse factors are unnecessary travel; poor supervision, estimating and planning, and scheduling; unsuitable tools and supplies; and lack of preventive maintenance. This detailed information can augment the development of the improvement action plan.

Unfortunately, work sampling is expensive and time consuming. Therefore, before such a study is commissioned, a maintenance management program review should be conducted to determine whether a work study is warranted.

SUMMARY

The scope of items covered by a program review and effectiveness rating requires extensive knowledge and familiarity with the concepts and practical applications of operations and maintenance management systems. Results of the review identify problem areas for immediate attention and opportunities for further study. It is questionable, however, whether current plant management can conduct a review objectively. As such, I recommend that the task be assigned to an outside consultant—the job can be completed in a relatively short period of time and at modest cost. It can be a worthwhile investment prior to a more detailed study of management systems by work sampling.

Bibliography

Facilities Management: A Manual for Plant Administration, second edition. Alexandria, Va.: Association of Physical Plant Administrators of Colleges and Universities, 1989.

Kaiser, Harvey H. *The Facilities Manager's Reference.* Kingston, Mass.: R. S. Means Company, Inc., 1989.

Kaiser, Harvey H., and Applied Management Engineering. *The Maintenance Management Audit.* Kingston, Mass.: R. S. Means Company, Inc., 1991.

Chapter 6

Productivity Through Privatization

John T. Hackett
Managing General Partner
CID Venture Partners, L.P.

The inclination of public institutions to administer a wide range of services is steeped in tradition. But, just as municipalities across the country have found that they can better meet their budgetary and societal obligations if services such as ambulance, fire protection, and hospital are provided by outside suppliers, colleges and universities may also find privatization a way to cut costs without cutting services. In this chapter, John Hackett illustrates how privatization of services can save colleges money.

During the 1980s, while U.S. manufacturers were being forced to respond to the pressure of foreign competition by improving productivity and reducing costs and prices, the service sector—of which higher education is a part—was posting price increases that greatly exceeded the broader measures of inflation. High prices in postsecondary education can be attributed to a number of realities: it is labor intensive, there are few substitutes for it, it is always in demand regardless of the cost, and it is relatively dependent on vertical integration for management techniques and structure. But this last, hiring and maintaining full-time employees, may be more amendable than previously believed possible. By reducing reliance on vertical integration and moving toward privatization—contracting with independent providers for needs ranging from professional staff to manual labor—service requirements can be met efficiently and with greater cost effectiveness.

The pressure for cost reduction that exists in a competitive business environment is not commonly found in higher education. Within the business arena there is usually an incentive system that rewards cost reduction techniques and improved financial performance. It is unusual to find a college or university that aggressively seeks and rewards improved productivity and cost-saving plans. University faculty and staff customarily respond to attempts to improve productivity with suspicion and hostility. As a result, little attention has been given to it or to reducing costs, and efforts to privatize have been considered unfair or opportunistic. But the rising cost of higher education has attracted much attention and criticism recently, and college and university administrators are beginning to realize that they must explore opportunities for cost reduction and develop techniques to improve productivity.

THE ROOTS OF VERTICAL INTEGRATION

The reliance on vertical integration by colleges and universities can be traced to several influences. Hiring practices at a public institution may reflect those of its state or local government. On some campuses, paternalism plays a role. A university that was unable to find and hire independent suppliers in its early years may be entrenched in a tradition of hiring and training its own staff. On-campus employment for students may be a means of providing financial aid. And, because of accounting practices, the costs of services undertaken by inside staff often appear lower than they actually are when compared to the fees charged by outside contractors.

The inclination of public institutions to administer a full range of services may be an outgrowth of state and local government policies that traditionally have integrated and increased the number of public employees. Historically, state and local governments have been reluctant to allow private organizations to provide public services. For instance, it is only recently—and in relatively few locales—that governments have permitted outside suppliers to manage fire protection organizations, correctional institutions, and public health services.

In regard to paternalism, on campuses where several generations of families have been employed, it is not uncommon for administrators to refer to a "bond of loyalty" between the university and the staff. In those instances, a proposal that would displace employees by using an outside supplier may be unacceptable to the administrators, regardless of the potential cost savings.

In addition, policies that favor the use of inside staff can be traced to the need to provide financial assistance. Although it is no longer a common practice, many colleges and universities have used campus employment as a kind of financial aid for students.

Also, when assessing the costs of a particular service, the use of inside staff may appear lower than the use of an independent contractor because the full cost of maintaining a staff is not always apparent. Where vertical integration exists, the fixed-cost portion of a service—such as wages and employee benefits—may be accounted for in other broader categories, while a private vendor's fee usually represents the full cost of a particular service.

OPPORTUNITIES FOR PRIVATIZATION

Consider the number and diversity of auxiliary enterprises that exist on many residential campuses. They include food services, cleaning and maintenance, student aid, cash disbursement, student records, and housing. It is possible that through privatization the costs of such services can be lowered and their quality improved. What follows are examples of how privatization can be accomplished.

Food Services

Colleges and universities can contract with nationwide food service companies to provide campus food services. In this way, an institution may reduce costs and avoid the administrative expenses associated with the direct management of food-service employees and facilities. Lower food-service costs are possible because the nationwide companies, which have lower unit costs as a result of a significantly larger volume of foodstuffs and lower fixed costs, pass the savings on to the institutions.

Cleaning and Maintenance

Productivity improvements can also be realized where private firms are hired for cleaning and maintenance services. These private contractors are often small entrepreneurial organizations that provide closer supervision of employees and use more cost-effective techniques than university staff do in those jobs.

Student Aid

Some of the more sophisticated services that universities provide are excellent candidates for privatization. For example, large institutions that maintain student financial assistance and loan programs can opt to have those services provided by private financial businesses. Through the application of sophisticated computer programs and high-speed computers, the unit cost of disbursement and collection of information and records can be reduced dramatically.

Cash Disbursement

Another service that universities may elect to permit outside vendors to provide is cash disbursement. By inviting local financial institutions to place automatic teller machines (ATMs) at several on-campus locations, the need for check-cashing services may be eliminated. Not only are the costs of staff, office space, negative float, and returned checks eradicated and abrasive relationships with students terminated, but agreements can be negotiated whereby the participating financial institutions pay fees to the student financial aid fund based on the volume of activity at their ATMs.

Student Records

Current technological advances can be applied to improve productivity on campus. For example, personal information that students are asked to provide frequently can be encoded on a combination identification/smart-credit-debit card. The technology can be provided by private vendors and would produce significant savings by eliminating duplicate record keeping, streamlining information retrieval and distribution, and reducing costs associated with the collection of tuition and fees.

Housing

Large residential universities can elect to enter into management/ maintenance contracts with or to sell housing facilities outright to hotel chains, which would then manage and maintain student housing. Either scenario would relieve an institution of the cost and administration of student housing and permit it to focus on its primary mission—teaching and research. The contract between the parties could require the managers to enforce university regulations regarding student conduct and allow the university to maintain student guidance and counseling programs within the dormitory system.

Other auxiliary services that are possible targets for privatization include campus retail stores, medical services, transportation, security, personal services, communications systems, recreation, entertainment, and intercollegiate athletics. Including private vendors as alternative means of providing specific services can allow the administration of a college or university to compare and evaluate the costs, quality, and scope of services. Without comparative data, it is difficult to evaluate the relative efficiency of vertical integration. Moreover, the resources that are currently devoted to the management of these enterprises might be used more productively in supporting the primary purpose of the institution.

PRIVATIZATION THROUGH PART-TIME FACULTY

While the preceding proposals may not be greeted with widespread enthusiasm, an interesting example of improving productivity through privatization—already in place on many campuses—is the growing use of part-time faculty. By employing part-time faculty, a significant portion of the fixed costs associated with full-time faculty is avoided. Part-time faculty are usually compensated on the basis of the number of hours taught, are not entitled to participate in employee benefit programs, and are not eligible for tenure or sabbatical leave. In addition, their presence at a university does not require as much support (i.e., secretaries and office space) as full-time faculty.

Generally, people elect to teach part-time in order to earn incremental income and/or maintain academic credentials. Consequently, they may be willing to teach evening and early-morning classes—schedules that full-time faculty are often reluctant to accept. And, it is possible that the flexibility to schedule classes at these times could help to increase enrollment, particularly among nontraditional students, and achieve higher classroom utilization rates. By increasing enrollment and classroom utilization, the associated fixed costs may be spread over a larger base, which ultimately reduces average and marginal costs.

A faculty comprised predominantly of part-time professors may not be feasible at every institution. Colleges and universities that place a high value on research, for example, would not benefit from such a configuration. Nevertheless, on many campuses the productivity, or cost/output ratio, of part-time faculty would likely be much higher than it is of full-time faculty. However, cost/output ratios aren't readily used to evaluate faculty performance or physical facility utilization rates.

SUMMARY

Attempts to achieve improved productivity through privatization of university services is not without risk, and the concept does not have universal applicability. But the potential rewards appear to significantly outweigh the risks. At minimum, selective application of privatization can result in a better understanding of comparative cost and efficiency. It may also result in improvements in productivity and more efficient use of increasingly scarce resources.

Chapter 7

Managing Technology Transfer

Edward L. MacCordy
Associate Vice Chancellor for Research
Washington University

University research has been responsible for many discoveries that have benefited society. Successful delivery of a useful product or process to the public requires coordinated efforts among the academic investigator, the university, and industry. Edward L. MacCordy discusses the aspects of a productive technology transfer program and points out how such a system can benefit institutions, industry, and the general public.

The transfer of university-developed technology to the commercial sector for conversion into products has become a voluntary commitment on the part of academia, the result of the university/government research-based and the university/industry technology-based relationships that have continuously evolved since the end of World War II. These relationships are far from static, and, given today's changing marketplace and the need for improved productivity, it is important to refine strategies for technology transfer and develop new methods as necessary.

In the late 1940s, an unwritten social contract was begun between universities and the federal government whereby a university would produce material benefits for society and the national economy in return for major federal financing of academic research. For many years, technology transfer was accomplished primarily through research results being published in scholarly journals, graduate students becoming scientists in the private sector, and academic researchers acting as consultants to industry. Transferring technology by patenting and licensing inventions was a minor activity conducted at only a few institutions. By and large, university research faculties were isolated from the commercial world and preferred the ivory-tower ambience over direct involvement with corporate America.

Today, without compromising its valued objectives of education, research, and public service, academia has changed its attitude concerning relations with industry. In a timely editorial in *Higher Education and National Affairs,* Peter W. Likins, president of Lehigh University, observed:

> Our very mission is undergoing a transformation that may alter forever the structural metaphor (ivory tower) for the American university. . . .
> The assimilation of universities into the mainstream of society did not happen by accident; it has been the result of powerful economic forces.
> We have been asked to help solve societal problems because of a real need for help, not because of our love of knowledge. At the same time that we are assisting our friends in the real world, we are trying to protect our own resources and make improvements in teaching and research. From both perspectives, the driving forces behind our changing role have been financial.

What technological benefits do our universities have to contribute to society? Research in genetic engineering has produced new medicines, better agricultural crops, and improved livestock. Mapping the human genome is leading to greatly improved diagnoses of genetic disorders, a new understanding of the causes of disease, new therapies to control diseases that were considered incurable a few years ago, and gene therapy to correct genetic defects. University research is leading to the creation of new ceramics and other new materials. Ongoing research is developing the potential use of superconductivity in transportation, power transmission, electronics, and other fields. The list is endless.

The formula for successful technology transfer involves creating incentives for the academic investigator, the university, and industry to deliver the benefits of their discoveries to the public. Investment to facilitate commercialization of discoveries is also part of the equation. At a university, investment is in the form of a scientist's ideas, energy, and time. University scientists are seldom motivated by the prospect of personal financial gain or the meager professional recognition commercialization of a discovery produces. They simply seem driven to respond to a need they can fill and by the knowledge that there is a receptive technology transfer process that will make their discovery available to those who can use it.

In addition to its investment in intellectual property, a university must also invest financially in the operation of its technology transfer program. This usually consists of funding the expenses of the few employees who conduct the activity plus travel, office support, and legal fees. It is generally hoped that licensing income will offset these expenses and that a major portion will be left over for distribution to the creators of the technology and to the institution to further its education and research programs.

In part, a university's motivation to invest in technology transfer comes from its sense of obligation to the public to deliver the benefits of research that is financed primarily with public funds. Recently, universities—as rich potential sources of technology—have felt an obligation to participate in state and regional economic development programs, as well as to contribute to American industry's competitiveness in the international marketplace. Another element is the hoped-for financial gain from sharing in the commercial success of faculty-created technology.

In order to convert the technology that it licenses into a commercially profitable product or process, industry must make a major risk investment. The cost of developmental research, scale up, production, regulatory approvals, and marketing constitutes a risk investment that needs to be justified by reasonable prospects for a large, sustained, and profitable advantage in the marketplace as a result of holding exclusive proprietary rights.

DEVELOPING A TECHNOLOGY TRANSFER PROGRAM

The strategy employed in the operation of a technology transfer program and the allocation of resources to it must be cost effective. Many existing programs were created without a thorough understanding of the economics of such activities, and they continue to operate without concern for cost effectiveness. In actual fact, there are many ways a technology transfer strategy can be developed—alternatives that are prime determinants of a program's productivity and cost effectiveness. However, an effective program will not guarantee the creation of profitable inventions or a high level of net licensing income but will encourage the creation of new technology and, if operated on a cost-effective basis, achieve optimum financial results.

The Transfer Unit

The most fundamental choice a university faces when developing a technology transfer program is the amount of resources it is willing to invest in the operation of the transfer unit. Obviously, the amount invested determines the makeup of the unit. Generally speaking, a university can choose from four alternatives.

The first alternative is to assign technology rights to research sponsors or to inventors and not have a transfer program. While this alternative costs little (there are the costs of processing disclosures and assignments), it is not a socially acceptable position for a university to take, unless its level of technology-transfer activity is very low.

The second alternative, one that also involves minimal investment by a university, is to use an outside organization to provide transfer services. The best-established organization of this type is the Tucson-based Research Corporation Technologies (RCT), which will provide patent management services to any university. For 40 percent of any related royalty income, RCT will screen a university's invention disclosures, determine which inventions are acceptable on the basis of commercial viability, and pay all patent and licensing costs. "Captured" patent management organizations, whose services are available only to designated universities, are also included in this category. One such is the University of California Patent Office, which serves institutions in the University of California System. Another is the Wisconsin Alumni Research Foundation (WARF), which serves the University of Wisconsin exclusively but is not owned, controlled, or financed by it.

The third alternative is to establish a specific in-house technology transfer program as part of a university's research administration function—such as the University of Pennsylvania, the University of Rochester, and Washington University have done. This strategy assures coordination between contracts for industrial research and licensing technology to industry.

The fourth alternative is simply to establish a separate technology transfer unit within the administrative structure of a university—a choice Stanford, MIT, and Harvard, among others, have made. With this alternative, the separation of the administration of industry-based research from technology licensing requires good coordination and cooperation.

The costs of these alternatives to universities vary from almost nothing to millions of dollars. For example, the minimum the fourth alternative would cost is $100,000 per year. The second alternative can be used in combination with any of the other three provided the external patent management firm does not insist on exclusivity. For high levels of activity, an on-campus unit is the preferable choice since the effectiveness of technology transfer depends on frequent personal contact with faculty, which can be easily provided by in-house staff. The independent on-campus unit, alternative four, is likely to be more expensive than alternative three and should be accompanied by means to ensure good relations with the research administration unit. The advantages this alternative provides over the third are greater abilities to hire well-qualified licensing specialists and to deal with a large volume of technology.

Identifying Marketable Technology

The next decision to be made when adopting a transfer strategy is how to encourage faculty members to disclose their discoveries. One way to create an interest in technology transfer and encourage the written disclosure of all potentially patentable discoveries is to conduct patent awareness activities focused on science and engineering faculty. There are problems with this approach, however. First, many investigators are likely to be reluctant to report discoveries. And second, it is difficult to separate discoveries that may be commercially viable from those that definitely are not. The evaluation of discoveries and the rejection of those that have a low probability of success is a delicate, speculative, and labor-intensive process and can consume a significant portion of a technology transfer unit's time—time more productively spent on licensing commercially viable technologies. It is possible to take a targeted approach to finding potentially worthwhile discoveries. Such an approach can be considerably more cost effective than the indiscriminate solicitation of disclosures. In addition, a targeted approach can overcome faculty reluctance to initiate invention disclosure and can find technology in early stages of development. Such targeting requires knowledge of ongoing research and reasonable appreciation of the commercial potential of research products. Early-stage identification often creates an opportunity to acquire support for further research from prospective licensees.

Funding developmental research. Funding developmental research to advance a fairly raw discovery to the stage where there is substantial proof of its practical utility is an important issue. Developmental research can make a discovery more appealing to potential licensees who are skeptical of claims of utility based on a few limited experiments. As desirable as such additional research is, however, financing it can be a major obstacle. Existing funds available to a researcher often do not accommodate additional investigation, and the original scope of a project may not allow it.

Various possibilities to acquire additional funding exist and should be explored by the technology transfer unit and/or the research administration staff on behalf of the faculty member inventor. All options depend, of course, on the raw technology's potential as a promising property. Among the funding sources are special federal programs such as the Small Business Innovative Research (SBIR) program offered by the National Science Foundation, the Department of Energy, the Department of Defense, the National Aeronautics and Space Administration, and others. Such funding must be requested by a small business (generally less than 500 employees) that has been promised an exclusive license by a university in return for developing the technology. The SBIR funding is channeled to a university via subcontract from a small business. In addition, funds from state economic development programs may be available to a university, although they usually require an in-state company cosponsor. However, the most common source of funding is sponsorship by a private company in return for an exclusive license commitment.

Two distinct institutional objectives are served by acquiring outside support for developmental research. First, one of the primary functions of universities, the conduct of research, is furthered. Second, by increasing the chances of successful transfer, the public service mandate is also advanced. As such, funding research that enhances technology transfer should be considered as part of the financial strategy for managing intellectual property.

The desire for support for developmental research is growing among research universities. Several have recently established a specific fund for this purpose, and others are thinking of doing the same. In the past, the status quo had been for the marketplace to select discoveries that merited development and then provide research funding. But the new, aggressive push to finance developmental research finds universities creating blind pools of money to be used for this purpose. With these pools, selection of discoveries for development is driven by in-house decisions, not necessarily by objective input from the marketplace. Among the sources of funding for them are private investors, including alumni and generous friends of a university; venture capital organizations; and major corporations—all having expectations of reasonable returns on their investment.

The risks associated with funding of this kind are obvious. By becoming involved in profit-making activities designed to benefit investors financially, a university assumes a fiduciary responsibility to those investors and risks not only a blot on its name and reputation if the development fails but also confusion and disappointment in the minds of some of its primary benefactors. In addition, use of such funds imposes a priority claim on licensing income—a claim that is likely to reduce the proceeds flowing to the inventor and his or her university's research and education programs.

Protecting Discoveries

Another issue that must be addressed when developing a technology transfer program is establishing proprietary rights under patent and copyright laws. The legal right to exclude others from making, using, or selling an invention is the essence of successful licensing. Some companies spend large amounts to file and prosecute patent applications for their own inventions even though the majority never make it to the marketplace. The expense is viewed as a cost of doing business—part of a company's investment in its future.

Similarly, universities must also obtain legal protection for the technology their researchers produce. Because rights so established can lead to a dominant market position, industry is usually interested in licensing such protected university technology. But every invention should not and cannot be patented. For example, an invention may turn out to be unpatentable—a status that can only be determined by filing and processing a patent application. And, when a patent is granted, there is no guarantee that the invention will be commercially viable. Only about one in ten patented inventions is ever commercialized. In addition, a market may include more than one country, and legal protection to cover it may require filing applications in each country. A conservative estimate is that a single U.S. patent costs at least $5000 and each foreign counterpart costs at least $3000.

Industry may be able to absorb such expenses, but universities cannot. For a university the issue is how to screen out inventions that are not likely to produce income and get potential licensees to pay for patenting those that are. A university should not invest in speculative patents with hope that they will serve as an incentive to attract licensees. Too often the consequence of such speculation is the accumulation of a sizable and expensive portfolio of issued patents that no one wants to license.

A more cost-effective strategy for a university is to rely on the marketplace to determine the commercial viability of inventions and to pay for patenting costs. This is not a risk-free strategy, however, but one that seeks to minimize financial risk and operating costs. It requires marketing inventions to licensees as early in the developmental phase as possible and convincing them to pay patenting expenses in return for exclusive commercial rights. (An indication of lack of commercial viability is that after a reasonable marketing effort, no licensee is found.)

Under this strategy a licensee may assume primary responsibility for preparation, filing, and prosecution of patent applications in the name of a university. Although some object to the practice because of the licensee's potential conflict of interest, many believe that a licensee is generally more knowledgeable about existing patent positions in its industry and can better determine the strongest and broadest attainable, defendable, and commercially useful set of patent claims to cover an invention than a university. Furthermore, through its own additional research and development efforts or by demonstrating a need for further development of experimental evidence by a university inventor, the licensee can contribute to a stronger patent position than the university would have by itself.

Thus, a strategy of cooperation and collaboration with licensees can increase the effectiveness of technology transfer and reduce costs to universities. In the process, licensees can contribute superior knowledge of world markets and of patent laws of foreign countries as well as add to the quality of patent applications.

Because of statutory time limits on filing domestic and foreign patent applications, this strategy must be used within strict time constraints. Occasionally, proper marketing cannot be done before a filing, and a speculative patent application may become necessary. Under these circumstances, it may be desirable to risk the cost of filing a speculative application rather than permanently lose rights to a potentially valuable invention.

Enforcing patent rights. Another major area of financial risk in technology transfer is the cost of legal services to defend the validity of a patent and enforce exclusionary rights. This litigation is so expensive that, except for a few very special cases, universities cannot justify it. The cost far exceeds typical licensing income. Among the exceptions are Stanford, which has used a portion of the royalties from the Cohen-Boyer patents on genetic engineering to build a fund to defend and enforce those patents. The Wisconsin Alumni Research Foundation and the Massachusetts Institute of Technology have also very selectively undertaken such litigation. Were it not for other enforcement alternatives, infringers could ignore university patent rights and make the licenses worthless.

The enforcement alternatives include conveying to exclusive licensees the right to defend the patent in litigation and requiring nonexclusive licensees to share in the cost of any patent litigation that serves their market interest. The exclusive licensee is motivated to litigate to preserve patent rights in order to protect its market position. In nonexclusive relationships, the university retains the right to litigate its patent but legal fees are paid by the licensees, who also want to protect their market positions.

Risking product liability. Another type of litigation that threatens universities concerns product liability. This is especially true for universities as they increasingly license the technology they have developed in-house to an advanced stage, often in collaboration with small companies or with start-ups in which they hold equity. (Such activities may indicate that universities are involved in commerce as opposed to their previous passive role as simple licensers.) Until recently, universities have felt secure with indemnification by established corporations. But, with an increase in bankruptcies, these corporations may no longer have the financial strength to indemnify universities against the threat of product liability—indemnification by a company that does not possess adequate financial resources is no protection at all. These factors plus the deep pocket character of well-endowed institutions increase the risk of universities being targeted for product liability litigation.

The only recent example of product liability litigation involved university-developed technology from the University of Wisconsin. In the late 1980s, WARF was named as a codefendant in a product liability suit in which the plaintiff sued for over $80-million as a result of being harmed by an invention developed at the university. WARF ultimately settled out of court. If WARF had not been the licensing agent for the university, the institution itself would probably have been named as a defendant.

In the future, if a major case against a university appears, it will send a clear warning to all universities—especially private institutions with large endowments—of the serious financial risk they are exposed to by their conduct of technology transfer activities. Considering the modest licensing income technology transfer generates at most universities, it would not be surprising if governing boards then terminated transfer activities rather than risk major expense and potential loss in product liability litigation. Clearly, stemming the flow of university technology would not be in the best interest of society.

Universities and their legal counsel should explore new alternatives for lessening the risk of product liability litigation. At least two come to mind. The first is to withdraw from the conduct of technology transfer activities and turn the function over to an outside patent management firm. The second is to arrange for closely affiliated but independent organizations to conduct the activities that might invite product liability claims. The relationship between WARF and the University of Wisconsin is one model of this. With the evolution and growth of technology-based relationships between universities and industry, the threat of product liability must be considered when developing a technology transfer program.

Multiple Methods of Transfer

The final component of a technology transfer strategy is the set of alternative mechanisms that provides for effective transfer. Too often technology transfer is perceived as a fixed course of action, i.e., the disclosure of inventions by investigators and the negotiation of licenses with established corporations. This oversimplification tends to perpetuate unimaginative, albeit busy, licensing programs and unnecessarily limits the interests and activities of the technology transfer manager.

Opportunities for conversion into a commercial product or process should be available for every new discovery. Discoveries need to be shepherded into the channels that can nurture them and match them with appropriate licensees. These channels are varied and include

- sponsorship of the development of a discovery by a company that (usually) would receive an exclusive license;
- sponsorship of research to produce new technology by a company or consortium that would be granted any licenses;
- sponsorship of basic or developmental research by a state economic development program, usually in conjunction with a company that wants to license the product of the research;
- collaborative research between a university and a small business under one of the federal Small Business Innovative Research programs, through which the small business would receive a license to commercialize the results;
- licensing technology on an exclusive, field-of-use exclusive, or non-exclusive basis;
- management of an invention by a technology management firm; and
- exclusive licensing by a specialized affiliate or venture capital organization that would use the discovery it has licensed as the basis for a start-up company.

Several of these alternatives require coordination between the research administration and technology transfer units if they are separate. There should be a strong, cooperative working relationship between the two.

Creating a start-up company. The last bulleted item in the preceding section is worth special mention. The use of university discoveries for the creation of start-up companies is an attractive option for many reasons but requires capabilities and funding that most universities do not have.

The main attraction of start-ups is that they provide alternative outlets for technology that might not otherwise be of interest to established corporations. It is rare for university technology to open up a market for a new product or process whose sales will significantly affect the bottom line of a large corporation. Considering development time and cost and compliance with state or federal regulations, even small companies may have mixed feelings about taking on the additional work of bringing a new product to market if it will be in competition with other ongoing company projects. But for a start-up, the university technology is its only project, its sole chance to make it big. Also, start-ups need to begin small and grow; they are satisfied with a product that fills a solid market niche. So, start-ups can be attracted by and devote all their energy to technology that may be less appealing to established companies.

Start-ups are attractive to universities for other reasons as well. In lieu of or in addition to royalties, it is common for a university to take equity in the start-up to which it has licensed technology. Royalties represent a percentage of the present value of a particular product in the marketplace and the value of equity is measured by the future valuation of a company and the prospects of all of its product lines. Equity does not depend completely on the maintenance of patent rights, as royalties usually do, although its value may be affected by a loss of such rights if sales suffer. When comparing the return from a technology's royalties with the value of equity in the company that licenses that technology, it is generally believed that the value of the royalties over time will be a small fraction of the value of the equity. Start-ups are also appealing because they can be a tangible contribution to the local and regional economy.

Creating a start-up, however, is not something a university can generally do on its own. It requires undertaking market research, developing a business plan, recruiting a management team, raising risk capital, and many other activities that university personnel have no experience with or proficiency in. To acquire such capabilities, universities have formed alliances of various kinds with outside organizations. In the excellent article "Options for Technology Transfer," published in the July 1989 issue of *Capital Ideas,* Richard Anderson and Barry Sugarman examined the use of "corporate affiliates for technology transfer" (CATT) as intermediaries between universities and start-up companies. According to the article, there are two options for establishing a CATT: a university can set up and finance a CATT itself, in whole or in part, or it can form an alliance with an organization, say a venture capital company, that is willing to finance and provide the necessary services in return for equity positions in each start-up. While the latter option may have financial advantages, it has obvious disadvantages: universities are left with limited control, and venture capital participants can be difficult to find. (Start-ups are high-risk investments, often described as pre-seed or seed capital deals, and most venture capital firms do not get involved in such early-stage investments.) Nevertheless, if costs to a university can be controlled and its research program is very productive, it may desire to have more than one CATT, since each has a limited field of interest and limited resources to devote to start-ups.

SUMMARY

Technology transfer at a typical research university has evolved over the last two decades without much thoughtful planning and design. Although it is generally acknowledged that technology transfer will be a small source of income, its existence is important to the research and public service objectives of higher education. It is an effective and essential means through which the benefits of university research are made available to society. It is also the primary means through which universities can contribute to local and regional economies and to the nation's competitive position in the global marketplace.

The potential drain on the financial resources of a university from a poorly conceived technology transfer program is almost unlimited. Institutions need to achieve maximum productivity at minimum financial risk through the development of cost-effective technology transfer strategies. To accomplish that, every element of a technology transfer program needs to be evaluated. The resulting strategy should be one that, at minimum, clearly defines an institution's plan for administration of the program, detects and develops new technology, establishes and defends proprietary rights to that new technology, avoids involvement in catastrophic litigation, and pursues multiple means for transfer to be accomplished. Such a strategy can only benefit the faculty, the university, the community, the country, and society at large.

Chapter 8

Higher Education and Efficient Resource Allocation

John H. Pencavel
Professor, Department of Economics
Stanford University

Most analysts acknowledge that higher education has exerted an influence on the United States economy, but the extent to which this can be judged has been hard to define. Examining the contributions of an educated work force to the nation's productivity, John Pencavel looks at how trends in education are effected by the economy and warns of the implications of a sustained economic slowdown on education.

No serious evaluation of higher education in the United States can be undertaken without an awareness of how the system operates within the context of the economy as a whole. In studying this relationship, two principal issues arise. The first concerns the role that higher education has played in the country's productivity slowdown. Quantifying education's part in this slowdown is not a straightforward task. The education system is but one of many factors that affect the organization and productivity of resources in the national economy. Indeed, it is because so many other factors contribute to economic growth and efficiency and because changes within these factors typically correlate with changes taking place throughout the education system that it is difficult to identify education's role precisely.

The second issue relates to the effectiveness of the higher education system in responding to changes in the needs and wants of the economy. How can one evaluate the performance of higher education in facilitating eco-

I am grateful to Richard E. Anderson and William F. Massy for their helpful comments on earlier versions of this essay.

nomic growth and technological change? What criteria can be applied to assess the education system's contribution? Using these criteria, does the higher education system promote efficient allocation of resources, including those directed to economic growth?

The market system provides incentives for schools to furnish general skills and for individuals to acquire them. The mechanism for producing highly skilled labor is functioning well, and, as a result, the causes for the slowdown in the nation's economic growth are unlikely to be attributable to changes in higher education. Nevertheless, there are some important implications of this productivity slowdown for higher education. Decline in economic growth manifests itself through sluggish growth in family income, yet, in the 1980s, the monetary returns of a college education rose. This may help to explain why tuition costs have been able to rise so rapidly without college enrollment rates falling. If in the 1990s the returns of a college education should appear less attractive and tuition continues to rise at the rates witnessed in recent years, the finances of colleges and universities as well as their teaching and research activities may well come under scrutiny from politicians, legislators, and the general public.

EDUCATION AND THE PRODUCTIVITY SLOWDOWN

Since about 1973, economic growth rates around the world have fallen compared with the growth experienced in the preceding twenty-five years. According to Angus Maddison in "Growth and Slowdown in Advanced Capitalist Economies: Techniques of Quantitative Assessment," while U.S. labor productivity (in terms of gross domestic product per hour worked) grew 2.5 percent per year between 1950 and 1973, it increased only 1.0 percent per year between 1973 and 1984. Many explanations have been offered for this slowdown in the growth of productivity, including the abrupt increases in energy prices in the 1970s, the changing composition of output from goods-producing industries to services, and the breakdown of the Bretton Woods international monetary system that was based on fixed exchange rates. Some commentators have even drawn attention to the fact that the drop in the U.S. economic growth rate came a few years after student test scores in high schools and primary schools began to decline. In "Is the Test Score Decline Responsible for the Productivity Growth Decline?," John Bishop indicates that the temptation to draw causal inferences from this association has proved irresistible.

Because these and other factors came into play at approximately the same time, it is difficult to discriminate among the competing explanations. Looking beyond a single country's experiences and examining the growth of productivity across several countries provides an important additional dimension for identifying the role of the different elements. Economic growth rates throughout the world have fallen since 1973—sometimes by more than the factor experienced in the U.S. However, the same complex features often exist in other countries, so the difficulty of distinguishing the particular part played by education remains.

Though a finger has been pointed at primary and secondary schooling in the United States, there is no substantiated evidence to merit the argument that colleges and universities are responsible for the productivity slowdown in the U.S. This does not mean that higher education has no impact on the efficient allocation of resources (including those directed to economic growth). On the contrary, there is abundant evidence that the skills produced by higher education play a significant role in the pace of technological change. Some of this evidence is drawn from aggregative data and some is taken from the microeconomic working of the system.

At the aggregate level, it has become a common procedure to relate the proportional growth of an economy's total output over a period of time to its level of inputs, including the quantity and quality of labor. The education of the labor force is normally included in the quality dimension. Such growth accounting exercises usually accord an important role to schooling in the pace of economic growth. For example, in Maddison's authoritative research, schooling is estimated to have contributed 11 percent to the growth of output in the United States between 1950 and 1973 and 23 percent between 1973 and 1984. Higher education alone contributed almost 3 percent between 1950 and 1973 and almost 15 percent between 1973 and 1984. Higher education's role in economic growth has always been greater in the U.S. than in other major industrialized countries due to the fact that in America a larger fraction of people from all age groups enroll in colleges and universities. Maddison's estimates come from a large body of literature that suggests that the relationship of education to economic growth may have varied effects across countries and over time, but, measured by these growth accounting procedures, it has nonetheless made a substantial contribution.

At the microeconomic level, an educated decision maker is more likely to be informed of the direct contributions to output of each input and of the relative values of input and output prices. For example, in "Technical

Change, Learning, and Wages," Ann Bartel and Frank Lichtenberg report that in U.S. manufacturing industries in 1960, 1970, and 1980, more highly educated workers were employed in fields where the capital equipment (i.e., physical capital) was new. This association was especially strong in industries where research and development expenditures represented a large fraction of total sales. In other words, firms on the technological frontier have a greater demand for college-educated employees because individuals with more schooling are better able to absorb and follow instructions, take initiative and deal with unforeseen contingencies, and envisage and exploit new possibilities. This demand is manifested not only by employment patterns, report William Dickens and Lawrence Katz in "Interindustry Wage Differences and Industry Characteristics," but also by the fact that the wages of college-educated workers in relation to those with only a high school education are greater in those industries. Thus, rapid technological change is facilitated when workers have completed more schooling, and the benefits of research and development activities are enhanced when complemented by a well-educated labor force.

Many economists believe that when new technologies are introduced, physical capital tends to replace unskilled labor. Hence, as physical capital becomes less expensive to obtain and operate, there is a decline in the demand for unskilled labor. As the economy accumulates more physical capital, the argument goes, the demand for less-skilled labor falls and the demand for college-educated labor increases. In other words, the relative demand for college-educated labor increases in tandem with increases in the relative supply of such labor.

There is a general belief that the contribution of schooling to economic growth is to facilitate technological change. Not much is known, however, about the *particular* skills acquired in school that are most valuable on the job. Perhaps because mathematical skills are most relevant to the problem-solving situations in some work environments, there is, according to Bishop in "Why High School Students Learn So Little and What Can Be Done About It," some agreement that this ability is most associated with workers' productivity. At present, however, this is no more than conjecture. There is little hard evidence about what skills developed during one's schooling contribute the greatest to productivity on the job.

It has been proposed that the country's productivity slowdown could be mitigated or corrected by using higher education as a policy tool. I am skeptical of this suggestion. The links between the generation of new ideas in colleges and universities and the production of skilled manpower on the one hand, and the rate of economic growth on the other, are multiple and complex. Funneling more resources into higher education would have an uncertain impact on the pace of economic change. Moreover, where would those resources be taken from?

The probable consequences of the economic slowdown for higher education are difficult to assess. A slowly growing economy will have fewer resources to spend on various activities—higher education among them. The reduction in America's economic growth rate has resulted in harder times for higher education than during the 1950s and 1960s, which are now seen as the Golden Age of growth. These hard times will not be relieved by the federal government's chronic budget deficit—a situation that encourages deep skepticism of all forms of government spending and gives rise to the constant search for ways in which the private sector can support activities once funded by the government.

Offsetting these effects are factors that may offer higher education room for expansion. That is, the system of higher education might reap some returns if it is determined that reversing the productivity slowdown requires a substantially higher quality labor force or greater research and development expenditures by industry. Indeed, a number of commentators have urged the federal government to adopt an industrial policy through which the government would identify the areas of industry where America has an actual or potential advantage over other countries and promote active development of them. High-technology industries are often put forward as candidates for this special attention. If they were to become part of an industrial policy, then higher education (which is a complement to them) would also benefit. However, there is little sign that such an aggressive policy will be adopted, so for the foreseeable future higher education should not look to the federal government for any financial largess.

HIGHER EDUCATION'S EFFECTIVENESS IN THE ALLOCATION OF RESOURCES

Consider now the general issue of higher education's response to the changing needs of the national economy. At least two questions need to be addressed here: (1) Is the appropriate number of highly educated workers being produced and is their quality sufficient? (2) Is the composition of these workers appropriate (e.g., are enough engineers being produced relative to the number of lawyers)?

Some commentators draw an unfavorable assessment of how the higher education system works when they maintain that there is either a shortage or an excess of a particular type of skill. In the late 1950s it was common to hear that the United States suffered from a shortage of engineers. Ten years later those claims were replaced by claims of a surplus of engineers. In the late 1970s and early 1980s the diagnosis of a shortage of engineers was revived. Though it does not necessarily follow that the system of generating new skills is not working well, claims of shortages and surpluses are, in fact, often registered in a manner that suggests such criticism.

When assessing the market for physical capital, one might study whether investments are taking place in industries where sales are buoyant and product prices relatively high. If so, the productive capacity of those industries would be expanding while *disinvestment* would be taking place in industries where the demand for products is sluggish. If a similar posture is taken with respect to the market for human capital (labor skills), one might determine whether the prices of those skills (wages) vary in response to supply and demand, whether enrollment in college corresponds to the differential earnings of college graduates vis-a-vis high school graduates, and whether the number of specialized professionals increases with the incentives to become trained in a specialty area. The first issue to address is whether the earnings premium attached to a college education is fixed and invariant with respect to factors affecting the demand for well-educated labor.

The College Earnings Premium

There is little doubt that the college earnings premium is not fixed. Consider as evidence the earnings differentials for new entrants into the labor force—people who have not yet made personal investments of time and energy that might affect their earnings in specific jobs with particular firms. For those individuals, we get a clearer estimate of the contribution of their education to their wages. Such individuals have accumulated general human capital—skills that are useful to a number of different employers. With many sellers and many buyers, the conditions of a competitive market prevail.

Relevant information regarding the earnings premium of attending college is given in Table 1, which is drawn from Mary Lydon's research. The underlying data are from the censuses of 1940, 1950, 1960, 1970, and 1980 and from the 1986 Current Population Survey. The entries in Table 1 report, for white men and women who completed their schooling one to five years

TABLE 1
Proportionate Weekly Earnings Differentials Between Individuals with Sixteen and Twelve Years of Education Who Have One to Five Years of Market Work Experience.

Year	White Men	White Women
1940	0.77	0.99
1950	0.36	0.38
1960	0.49	0.60
1970	0.63	0.73
1980	0.48	0.58
1986	0.58	0.99

Notes: These figures are taken from Mary Lydon's "Movements in the Earnings/Schooling Relationship, 1940-86." They are transformations of ordinary least-squares regression coefficients attached to a dummy variable denoting sixteen years or more of schooling and where the reference category identifies those with twelve years of schooling. The dependent variable is the logarithm of weekly earnings. Other regressors include two other schooling dummy variables (one for zero to eleven years and one for thirteen to fifteen years) and dummy variables for years of experience. Actual years of experience are not known but are estimated by subtracting estimated age upon leaving school (defined as years of schooling plus six) from current age.

previously, the proportionate difference in earnings between college and high school graduates. The college earnings premium ranged from 36 percent to 77 percent for men and from 38 percent to 99 percent for women. In any given year, the earnings premium for new workers is higher for women than for men. The premium was relatively high in 1940, low in 1950, higher in 1960 and 1970, fell in 1980, and rose dramatically in the first half of the 1980s. This does not give the appearance of a fixed, immutable price. On the contrary, it suggests a variable wage differential.

A number of reasons for the variations in the college earnings premium in Table 1 have been offered. The figure for 1940 is probably affected by the lingering heavy unemployment of the 1930s depression: wage differentials between skill groups appear to widen as the general level of unemployment increases. The new labor market entrants studied in 1950 (i.e., those who entered between 1945 and 1949) were those whose schooling was affected, perhaps impaired, by World War II. If the quality of their college education suffered because of the war, one might expect a smaller premium for a college education, which was the case in 1950. The decline in the college premium during the 1970s (reflected in the figures for 1980) is usually attributed to the increased supply of new workers as baby boomers completed their formal schooling and entered the labor market. This increased supply of inexperienced workers came from all schooling levels, but more were college graduates. The premium's remarkable rise in the first half of the 1980s is less explainable. It may well be related to changes in industrial structure—changes that had been going on for years but accelerated and became more marked in that decade. There may also have been a shift in the relative demand for skilled labor as assembly-line jobs in durable-goods manufacturing industries declined and those in the advanced-technology sectors increased.

College Enrollments

Although evidence supports the notion that wage differentials between college and high school graduates vary over time in response to factors affecting their demand and supply in the work force, this conclusion raises the question of whether changes in the college earnings premium induce changes in college enrollment. This is difficult to assess because the earnings premium represents only one of a number of factors affecting college attendance. For example, there have been changes over time in the availability of government grants and loans to students that have affected the ability of individuals to obtain a college education. Also, in the late 1960s and early 1970s, the Vietnam War and the possibility of securing college deferments altered enrollment rates. Notwithstanding these complicating factors, as a fraction of those graduating from high school, the percentage of people enrolling in college fell from 35 percent in 1960 to approximately 31 percent from 1974 to 1980 and rose to 34 percent in 1984. In other words, though the picture is not always clear, the movement in college enrollment since the late 1960s seems to follow the movement in the college earnings premium, with larger wage differentials inducing an increased supply of college-educated labor.

As already indicated, if the higher education system produces skilled labor in response to market incentives, we should expect enrollment to be affected not only by the college earnings premium but also by the out-of-pocket expenses of a college education. That is, factors such as tuition and financial aid should affect enrollment, and existing research indicates that they do. In "The Demand for Higher Education," Michael McPherson examined ten studies of the effect of tuition on enrollment and "every single one finds a significant negative relationship between the net price faced by students and their probability of attending college." He estimates that, on average, a 10 percent increase in tuition reduces enrollment by 3 percent.

This relatively inelastic response is plausible given that the effect relates to a change in tuition for all colleges simultaneously. (A much larger decrease would be expected if tuition were raised at one college while tuition at all other colleges remained unchanged.)

In a thorough analysis of almost 23,000 high school seniors from the National Longitudinal Study of the high school class of 1972, Charles Manski and David Wise in *College Choice in America* found that students were very aware of tuition, scholarship, and alternative employment opportunities when deciding whether to go to college. They reported, "The students who did attend college were the most likely to benefit from college education by obtaining a degree." In other words, those who chose not to go to college tended to be those who would have been unlikely to have benefited from it in the first place. The same finding emerged from Robert Willis and Sherwin Rosen's study of 3,611 male World War II veterans, *Education and Self-Selection.* The researchers concluded, "If we examine a subpopulation of persons with given measured abilities . . . , the empirical results on selectivity imply that those persons who stopped schooling after high school had better prospects as high school graduates than the average member of that subpopulation, and that those who continued on to college also had better prospects there than the average member of the subpopulation." But monetary factors are not the only determinants of college enrollment—scholastic achievement at high school and parental schooling levels also affect one's decision to go to college, for instance. However, the role of monetary considerations is marked: Willis and Rosen estimated that a 10 percent increase in starting salaries would induce nearly a 20 percent increase in college enrollment. In general, the proposition that students respond to the pecuniary costs and benefits of attending college is supported by compelling evidence.

The Supply of Professional Manpower

The notion that college enrollment is directly affected by changes in tuition and starting salaries lies behind research that has tried to account for the movement of college students into different fields. Monetary costs and benefits represent the most visible part of the net return on a college education, so it is natural for researchers to look for associations between these monetary factors and the popularity of particular fields of study.

Table 2 presents the percentage of all master's, first professional, and doctoral degrees conferred in the major fields of study at regular intervals between the academic years 1949-50 and 1985-86. The data show that while the popularity of some fields follows strong continuing trends (upward in business and computer and information sciences, downward in other social sciences), cycles of growth and decline are evident in other fields. The relative number of degrees conferred in education rose in the mid-1950s, fell in the mid-1960s, rose again in the mid-1970s, and fell again in the mid-1980s. The relative number of degrees in law and medicine fell from the mid-1950s to the early 1970s but have risen since then. Engineering degrees increased in the mid-1960s, fell to a low point a decade later, and began to rise again in the 1980s.

There are essentially two ways to account for the fluctuations in degrees awarded and, in particular, for the suggestion that in several fields a cyclical pattern exists. The first looks for fluctuations in the independent variables that determine the relative costs and benefits of specializing in different fields. For instance, we would expect the incentive to acquire an education degree—a step toward becoming a primary or secondary school teacher—to be related to the projected demand for teachers as derived from the number of school-age children. These projections can be estimated from contemporary fertility rates and demographic profiles. The second explanation focuses on the internal dynamics of the market structure itself, noting the lag between the date individuals enroll in a college program and the date they graduate and enter the labor market. This lag implies that the costs and benefits of specializing in different fields are uncertain; individuals who enter a college program must estimate the labor market conditions they will face in the future. The ways in which they make these estimates determine the internally generated fluctuations in the number of new entrants to a profession.

It needs to be emphasized, however, that the source of new supplies of manpower to a profession does not consists exclusively of current graduates. In a number of cases a substantial fraction of new entrants are individuals returning to their profession after interrupting their career or entering a profession for the first time after obtaining the qualifications some time before. (This has become a more prominent feature of the professional labor market as women have made more determined efforts to reenter it after withdrawing for a time to take primary responsibility for the care of their young children.)

For example, 84 percent of new elementary and public school teachers in 1986 consisted of individuals who were not attending college or teaching in

TABLE 2
Master's, First Professional, and Doctoral Degrees Awarded by Field as a Percent of
All Such Degrees.

Degree	1949-50	1955-56	1959-60	1965-66	1970-71	1975-76	1980-81	1985-86
Business and Management		4.0	4.6	7.1	9.1	10.6	14.7	17.2
Computer and Information Sciences					0.6	0.7	1.1	2.1
Economics	1.3	0.9	0.9	1.0	0.9	0.7	0.7	0.7
Education	23.6	37.0	33.0	28.2	31.7	33.3	26.7	21.1
Engineering	5.5	6.2	7.5	8.4	6.7	4.7	4.8	6.3
English and Literature	2.8	2.7	3.1	3.7	3.5	2.1	1.5	1.5
Health Professions					2.0	3.1	4.2	5.0
Law (LL.B./J.D.)		9.6	8.7	7.0	5.0	7.9	9.1	9.0
Life Sciences		3.2	3.2	3.3	3.1	2.4	2.4	2.1
Mathematics	1.3	1.3	1.9	2.9	2.1	1.2	0.8	1.0
Medicine (M.D.)	6.3	7.9	6.6	4.0	3.0	3.3	3.9	4.0
Other Social Sciences					5.8	4.2	3.1	2.1
Physical Sciences		5.0	4.9	4.2	3.6	2.2	2.1	2.4

Notes: "Health Professions" includes hospital and health care administration, nursing, dental specialties, occupational therapy, pharmacy, dental hygiene, public health, veterinary medicine specialties, speech pathology, and medical laboratory technologies. "Life Sciences" includes anatomy, biochemistry, bacteriology, biology, botany, entomology, physiology, and zoology. "Mathematics" includes statistics. "Physical Sciences" includes astronomy, chemistry, geology, metallurgy, meteorology, and physics. "Other Social Sciences" includes anthropology, archaeology, history, geography, political science and government, sociology, demography, urban studies, and criminology. The fields listed represent three quarters of all master's, first professional, and doctoral degrees awarded in 1985-86. Before 1960-61, first professional degrees are not distinguished in the data from bachelor's degrees. For the years 1949-50, 1955-56, and 1959-60, therefore, I have estimated the total number of first professional degrees by assuming they represented the same fraction of the total (bachelor's and first professional degrees) as in 1960-61 (which was 0.0569).

The data are taken from issues of *Digest of Education Statistics,* National Center for Education Statistics, U.S. Department of Education, particularly the 1988 issue (CS88-600).

1985. In 1966, report Richard Murnane and Randall Olsen in "Will There Be Enough Teachers?," only 33 percent fell into this category. In the case of teachers, it appears as though an increase in salaries postpones the date at which they drop out (perhaps temporarily) of teaching. In particular, a $1,000 increase in annual salary (in 1987 dollars) extends the first spell of teaching by an average of over a year. Those teachers who score high on the National Teachers Examination (NTE) have shorter first spells as teachers, which may suggest that more attractive alternative opportunities are available to them than are available to teachers who score low on the NTE. In general, movements in the supply of professional manpower operate not only through the production of new graduates but also through changes in the rate of attrition of trained personnel and in the rate of reentry into the profession. These factors are rarely included in conventional projections of manpower requirements.

SUMMARY

The system for producing college-educated manpower responds to the needs of the U.S. economy. The routes through which these needs are expressed are the earnings differentials attached to skilled workers and the earnings premia awarded to particular occupational groups. These differentials are not fixed and are not invariant to changing features of the economy. On the contrary, the earnings differentials paid to new workers who have graduated from college display remarkable variation over time, as does the supply of college graduates. While some of these variations can be explained and understood after the fact, they are very difficult to forecast.

Yet forecasts are constantly being made. Take, for example, the academic labor market projections made in William G. Bowen and Julie Ann Sosa's book, *Prospects for Faculty in the Arts and Sciences.* They project that if current trends continue, serious shortages of university faculty will exist in the mid or late 1990s. These shortages would not be due to faculty retiring or leaving but to population trends affecting enrollment and, in particular, to the large number of students moving through elementary and secondary schools that will be arriving at college during this decade. Moreover, they conjecture that the faculty shortage will be apparent in the humanities and social sciences as well as in the natural sciences.

If Bowen and Sosa are correct, there are some important questions for college administrators and trustees to face, among them: should colleges try to mitigate these faculty shortages and, if so, how can it be accomplished?

While their book focuses on outlining the problems and not on policy responses, Bowen and Sosa recommend ameliorating the shortage by increasing financial assistance to graduate students and reducing the time required to finish doctoral programs. If their projections are correct, the general issue of the performance of the higher education system is likely to soon come under serious critical examination.

The problem in clearly identifying higher education's contribution to economic growth and the efficient allocation of resources arises from the fact that the education system not only influences the nation's economy but is also profoundly affected by it. Indeed, it is because higher education is closely integrated into the market economy that it is able to respond to changing economic needs. For instance, the computer and information revolution sweeping through industry has provided clear signals for students to acquire literacy in these skills, and there is no doubt that many colleges and universities have responded accordingly. The standard routes through which these signals are transmitted in a market economy are the earnings differentials attached to particular skills. As noted, such earnings premia are enjoyed not only by those individuals with more years of schooling but also by those working in industries that are experiencing rapid technological change. Firms in these industries are willing to pay a premium for well-educated workers because such employees are better at understanding and responding to new technologies.

However, the earnings premia attached to a college education and to particular occupations have not been fixed over time but have displayed quite marked movements. These changes imply that the returns to investment in higher education, both for individuals and for society at large, may be difficult to forecast with confidence. For example, when the college earnings premium is relatively high, the personal and social incentives to attend college and to expand public support for higher education will seem great. But, by the time individuals who based their decision to attend college on that earnings premium acquire college-taught skills, the returns may have fallen considerably.

This, of course, presumes that individuals tailor their schooling and occupational decisions in response to market rewards. If they did not, the signals generated by technological change would not induce resources to be allocated where they could command a premium. In fact, such supply responses are in evidence, and an informed public policy should understand how these processes work and should not frustrate their operation. Policies designed to compress and eliminate earnings differentials (e.g., those that apply the same salary scale to all teachers in a district regardless of the alternative opportunities of those trained in chemistry, physics, and mathematics) are likely to obstruct the operation of the market system that delivers scarce resources to those areas of the economy where they are most valued. Enlightened policies arise out of an understanding of the way in which skills are produced by the education system in a market economy.

Bibliography

Bartel, Ann P., and Frank R. Lichtenberg. "The Comparative Advantage of Educated Workers in Implementing New Technology." *The Review of Economics and Statistics,* vol. 69, no. 1 (February 1987): 1–11.

————. 1988. "Technical Change, Learning, and Wages." Working Paper 2732. National Bureau of Economic Research.

Bishop, John. 1988. "Why High School Students Learn So Little and What Can Be Done About It." Working Paper 88-01. Center for Advanced Human Resource Studies. New York State School of Industrial and Labor Relations, Cornell University.

————. "Is the Test Score Decline Responsible for the Productivity Growth Decline?" *American Economic Review,* vol. 79, no. 1 (March 1989): 178–97.

Bowen, William G., and Julie Ann Sosa. *Prospects for Faculty in the Arts and Sciences.* Princeton: Princeton University Press, 1989.

Dickens, William T., and Lawrence F. Katz. "Interindustry Wage Differences and Industry Characteristics." *Unemployment and the Structure of Labor Markets,* Kevin Lang and Jonathan S. Leonard, eds. New York: Basil Blackwell, 1987.

Killingsworth, Charles C. "Automation, Jobs, and Manpower." *Nation's Manpower Revolution.* Report of the Subcommittee on Employment and Manpower of the Senate Committee on Labor and Public Welfare. 88th Cong., 1st sess., 1963.

Lydon, Mary. "Movements in the Earnings/Schooling Relationship, 1940–86." Ph.D. diss. in progress, Stanford University, 1989.

Maddison, Angus. "Growth and Slowdown in Advanced Capitalist Economies: Techniques of Quantitative Assessment." *Journal of Economic Literature,* vol. 25, no. 2 (June 1987): 649–98.

Manski, Charles F., and David A. Wise. *College Choice in America.* Cambridge: Harvard University Press, 1983.

McPherson, Michael S. "The Demand for Higher Education." *Public Policy and Private Higher Education,* David W. Breneman and Chester E. Finn Jr., eds. Washington: Brookings Institution, 1978.

Murnane, Richard J., and Randall J. Olsen. "Will There Be Enough Teachers?" *American Economic Review,* vol. 79, no. 2 (May 1989): 247–52.

Willis, Robert J., and Sherwin Rosen. "Education and Self-Selection." *Journal of Political Economy, Supplement,* vol. 87, no. 5, part 2 (October 1978): 7–36.